T0244762

HOW TO TALK ABOUT LOVE

ANCIENT WISDOM FOR MODERN READERS

■ ■ ■ ■

HOW TO TALK ABOUT LOVE

■ ■ ■ ■ ■

An Ancient Guide for Modern Lovers

Plato

Selections from Plato's *Symposium*

Translated and Introduced by
Armand D'Angour

PRINCETON UNIVERSITY PRESS

PRINCETON AND OXFORD

Copyright © 2025 by Armand D'Angour

Princeton University Press is committed to the protection of copyright
and the intellectual property our authors entrust to us. Copyright
promotes the progress and integrity of knowledge created by
humans. Thank you for supporting free speech and the global
exchange of ideas by purchasing an authorized edition of this book.
If you wish to reproduce or distribute any part of it in any form,
please obtain permission.

Requests for permission to reproduce material from this work
should be sent to permissions@press.princeton.edu

Published by Princeton University Press
41 William Street, Princeton, New Jersey 08540
99 Banbury Road, Oxford OX2 6JX

press.princeton.edu

All Rights Reserved

ISBN 9780691256887
ISBN (e-book) 9780691268712

British Library Cataloging-in-Publication Data is available

Editorial: Rob Tempio and Chloe Coy
Production Editorial: Mark Bellis
Text and Jacket Design: Heather Hansen
Production: Erin Suydam
Publicity: Tyler Hubbert and Carmen Jimenez
Copyeditor: Lachlan Brooks

Jacket Credit: Peter Horree / Alamy Stock Photo

This book has been composed in Stempel Garamond LT Std
and Futura

Printed in the United States of America

1 3 5 7 9 10 8 6 4 2

CONTENTS

CONTENTS

INTRODUCTION: TALKING OF LOVE

How do we talk about Love? Love is about feelings, emotions, beliefs, and behaviors. It is a psychological phenomenon, an irresistible force, an indispensable part of life, and much more besides. It embraces ways of thinking and speaking that differ widely between individuals and cultures. Love poetry, songs, novels, and films—not to mention psychological and philosophical studies of love—all have their own ways of talking about it. In them we find love analyzed, dissected, admired, lamented, and otherwise depicted in a huge variety of ways. These depictions raise questions to which very different answers might be given.

Is love based on physical attraction? Is it a force for good behavior? How does it relate to sex? Does love make the world go round? Is love divine?

The ancient Greeks too had many different ways of talking about love, but their starting point was that love was, literally, divine: love was personified as the god Eros (Cupid to the Romans) or as the goddess Aphrodite (Venus). These deities are named early on in Greek literature, in the authoritative ancient catalogue of divine origins by the poet Hesiod, his *Theogony* (*Birth of the Gods*) composed around 700 BCE. In addition, the stories, words and expressions of the Greeks' foremost poet and literary influence, Homer, whose epics the *Iliad* and *Odyssey* were composed roughly contemporaneously with Hesiod, gave the Greeks clear points of departure for thinking and debating the meaning and workings of love.

Epic Love

Western literature begins with a love story, intertwined with a tale of heroism, strife, and death. The cause of the Trojan War, the conflict in the background of Homer's *Iliad*, was said to have been the Judgment of Paris. The myth tells how the Trojan prince Paris (also known as Alexander) was chosen to judge a contest between three goddesses to decide which of them was the most desirable. To win his approval, each goddess proposed gifts related to their respective realms. Hera, queen of the gods, offered to make him ruler of Europe and Asia; Athena, goddess of war and handicraft, offered him wisdom and skill in fighting; and Aphrodite offered him the love of the most beautiful woman on earth, Helen of Sparta. Paris awarded the prize to Aphrodite. Unfortunately, his reward, Helen, was already married to Menelaus, king of Sparta. After visiting the latter's palace, Paris ran away with Helen and took her back home with him to Troy—sparking endless debate in antiquity about whether he had abducted her by force or whether she fell in love with him and went willingly.

The perfidious "theft" of Helen by Menelaus's guest led the Greeks to mount an expedition to retrieve her under the leadership of Agamemnon, Menelaus's brother and the most powerful of the Achaean (Greek) rulers. The ten-year Trojan War that followed—waged for the sake of a woman, later Greeks incredulously remarked—ended with the destruction of Troy and the deaths of many great heroes on both sides, including Achilles, Patroclus, Hector, and Paris.

Love is not only the casus belli, but plays a significant role in the course of the war. Achilles, strongest of the Achaeans, withdraws in anger from battle after Agamemnon takes from him his captured, and cherished, concubine Briseis. He reenters the fray after his beloved friend Patroclus is killed by Hector, brother of Paris. Hector is killed, in turn, by Achilles, whose own death, which lies beyond the frame of Homer's *Iliad*, will take place soon afterward. Following the war, Helen is reunited with Menelaus in Sparta, as described by Homer in his other great epic, the *Odyssey*.

The *Odyssey* tells of the adventures of Odysseus in his journey back to his palace in Ithaca. Various kinds of love are described in the course of the story. On the magical islands of Calypso and Circe, Odysseus unabashedly enjoys the pleasures of sex. But his enduring affection for his clever and faithful wife Penelope makes him long to return, as eventually he does, to his home. The kind of loving partnership depicted between him and Penelope is also shown in the *Iliad* in the love of Andromache for her doomed husband Hector, as well as in the close comradely love that drives Achilles to avenge Patroclus.

In the *Odyssey*, even the love between human beings and animals is depicted. One of the most touching moments in the epic comes when Odysseus, returning from Troy and his travels, encounters his aged dog Argos, still alive but lying neglected on a dung heap. Odysseus is in disguise, but the enfeebled Argos recognizes him:

Though twenty long and dismal years
  had passed,
fate granted that he see his lord at last.
Now darkness falls upon his weary eyes:
he feebly wags his tail for joy, and dies.
             (adapted from the translation
                  by Alexander Pope)

In song, poetry, and fable, love and death are closely intertwined. The connection persists over the centuries, and emerges as a persistent theme in Plato's *Symposium*. Love seems bound to encounter death, but also has the power to transcend it.

Lyric Love

Homer's scenes and expressions provided a foundation for poets to elaborate their personal feelings and experiences of love in song and story. So it was throughout the "lyric" age of the seventh to sixth centuries BCE, so called because poets of the time generally sang their songs to the accompaniment of the lyre. One such poet, Mimnermus of Colophon, who flourished around 630 BCE, composed a song about love in elegiac verse (a form generally accompanied by the *aulos*, double-pipe):

> *What life or pleasure can there be*
> *when golden Aphrodite's gone?*
> *To die would be far preferable*
> *than living robbed of love's delights,*
> *the tender gifts of sex that make*
> *young men and women glow with joy.*

Over subsequent centuries, other lyric poets such as Anacreon of Teos and Alcaeus of Lesbos composed songs in which love was a memorable theme. One of the earliest and most outstanding representatives of lyric song was Sappho, a singer-songwriter from the island of Lesbos. Her love songs, many of which express desire and admiration for girls, were so haunting that an ancient author tells of the Athenian politician Solon, a contemporary of Sappho's, being so enchanted when he heard his nephew singing one that he exclaimed, "Teach me this song so that I may learn it and die!"

Sappho's songs have survived as evocative fragments of poetry, sometimes no more than single words or powerful phrases:

Love, the melter of limbs, convulses me
  once again,
  sweetbitter unmanageable thing,
    stealing over me (fragment 130)

Love shook my heart
like the wind on a mountain
  streaming over oak trees (fragment 47)

In these fragments, love is personified as Eros, the Greek word *erōs* from which "erotic" derives, signifying passionate love or desire and thus distinguishable from the kind of love one might feel for family and friends, which was designated in Greek by *philia*. Elsewhere, Sappho speaks of Aphrodite, whom she also calls by the name Kupris (goddess of Cyprus), as the personification of love.

In a song that survives in reasonably full form (fragment 16), Sappho draws a contrast between her tender feelings of love for an absent friend and the masculine passion for war and fighting:

Some say a troop of cavalry
or marching men, or ships of war,
the finest sight on this dark earth;
    I say it's who you love.

This proposition isn't hard
at all to prove; for Helen, far
the loveliest of womankind
   forsook the best of men,

and sailed across the sea to Troy
without a thought for those she'd left
behind, her child and husband dear,
   but unresisting she

was led by Aphrodite. See,
a mortal mind is lightly turned;
for me, it's Anactoria
   I think of, now she's gone.

I'd sooner see her lovely walk
and sunlight darting on her cheeks
than all those Lydian chariots
   and fighting-men at arms!

Sappho's allusion to Helen here links
the notion of love to the bittersweet cause

of the Trojan War. As Sappho's own epithet "sweetbitter" (*glukupikros*) in fragment 130 above indicates, love has the capacity to give both pleasure and pain—it can be something to lament as well as to celebrate. The duality of love was an ever-present notion for Greek authors; love was recognized to be the source not only of delight, but of tragedy.

Tragic Love

Love's dual nature was vividly explored in Greek tragic drama, the foremost poetic genre that flowered in Athens during the fifth century BCE. In Sophocles' tragedy *Antigone*, the chorus sings of the power of love, Eros. Love binds the ruler Creon's son Haemon to the heroine Antigone, whose opposition to Creon's decree will lead to the death of both (lines 781–800):

Eros, unconquerable in battle, Eros who
lays waste to wealth,
who spends the night on a girl's soft
cheeks,
and roams across the sea and through
the homes of country-dwellers,
no god escapes you, nor any mortal
whose life is but a day:
you create infatuation in all who
encounter you.

You capture the hearts of virtuous people
and turn them to ruin;
it is you who have incited this family
conflict.
Your victory is the desire that gleams in
the eyes of the sweet bride.
Desire is enthroned in power along
with the eternal laws,
when the goddess Aphrodite, irresist-
ible, plays her game.

In Euripides' *Hippolytus*, the chorus similarly recognizes the unrequited and illicit passion of the queen, Phaedra, for Hippolytus, and pleads with the god of love (lines 525–32):

Eros, Eros, distilling liquid desire on the eyes,
infusing sweet pleasure into the souls of those
against whom you aim your arrows,
never show yourself to me in anger,
never come but in harmony!

Neither the shafts of fire, nor of the sun,
are stronger than the arrows of Aphrodite
which Zeus's son Eros hurls from his hand.

Love was thus hymned by the dramatists as divine and unavoidable, intensely desirable yet potentially tragic. Eros is presented as an unstoppable force of nature, leading to powerful amorous entanglements that bring with them both the prospect of superhuman elation and the inevitability of sorrow.

Another kind of love, however, that of wife for husband, is the focus of an early play by Euripides, his *Alcestis* (438 BCE). King Admetus of Thessaly has been granted the privilege of living beyond his allotted lifespan if he can find someone to take his place. When his aged parents refuse to do so, his wife Alcestis nobly volunteers to die instead of him, saying that his death will leave her without a lover and their children without a father. The hero Heracles arrives at the palace and confronts Death, forcing him to release Alcestis from his grasp, whereupon she is restored to life and to her family. The tale is interpreted in the *Symposium* as showing that the gods accorded Alcestis special favor on account of the nobility she showed in being prepared to die in place of the man she loved.

The Background of the *Symposium*

Some love epigrams have been attributed to Plato himself, including a romantic effusion to a beloved youth called Aster ("Star," *Greek Anthology* 7.669):

> *You gaze up at the stars, my love. Could*
> *   I but, too,*
> *become the sky with all its eyes, to gaze*
> *   on you.*

More significantly, however, Plato wrote the earliest and by far the most famous prose contribution to the question of how love might be thought and spoken about:

the *Symposium*. Dating from around 380 BCE, the dialogue (the standard term used for the thirty-odd surviving works attributed to Plato, even though not all are in literal dialogue form) presents a fictional, semi-dramatic philosophical exploration of the notion of Eros. The dialogue is a masterpiece of design, ideas, and expression, and the only extended ancient treatment of the topic of love. Its literary brilliance and philosophical depth have been recognized since antiquity, and it is still widely read today.

Plato presents his ideas through the mouths of participants in a *symposion*, a drinking party. The party he describes takes place in the house of the playwright Agathon, after the latter has won first prize for his tragedy at a dramatic competition: the scene is therefore datable to 416 BCE. A number of people of whom we have knowledge from other contexts, including Plato's teacher Socrates and the comic poet Aristophanes, are present. We are asked to imagine a dining-room in which the participants are reclining on couches (we are told that others were present, but their speeches were omitted). They take turns in speaking according to the scheme shown in the diagram below.

The speeches start, then, with that of Phaedrus, and proceed counterclockwise. After some unreported speeches by unnamed symposiasts (partygoers), Pausanias speaks. The order is then disrupted because Aristophanes has a fit of hiccups and Eryximachus agrees to speak before him. Agathon then gives his speech, after which there follows a short exchange in which Socrates elicits from him some modifications to his

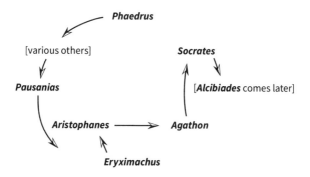

propositions. Thereafter, Socrates presents the doctrine of love that he attributes to a woman called Diotima. Finally, Alcibiades interrupts the proceedings and seats himself next to Agathon before proceeding to give the longest speech of all.

Each speaker offers a different perspective about what love might mean for human life and relationships from their point of view. It was common for educated elite men such as those depicted in the *Symposium* to be the lovers of younger men, or to have older men as lovers: the host Agathon and his older lover Pausanias are one such couple. Among the Greeks' accepted values was a demand to show courage in battle, to enjoy loyal friendships, and to demonstrate the ability to speak with eloquence and persuasiveness. The speeches of the symposiasts explore and demonstrate all these values in an expressly homoerotic context. This emphasis reflects the sociological reality. Women were peripheral to the social hierarchy of Athens; the only women present in a symposium would have been female slave entertainers (*aulētrides*) or elite sex workers (*hetairai*) with musical expertise, entertaining the male symposiasts and providing music on the pipes. On this occasion, we are told, the slave-pipers are sent away so that the men can stage their discussion.

The descriptions and notions of love expressed must be broadly understood within the homoerotic context depicted. However, they can offer the reader a more general understanding of what love might be thought to mean, and it's evident that Plato would have wanted the exploration of love to extend to heterosexual as well as homosexual relationships. The central contribution to the dialogue is delivered by Socrates, who reports the doctrine of love that he claims to have learned from a woman, Diotima. The pseudonym, with its clear meaning "honored by Zeus," points to a likely historical influence on Socrates' thinking, Aspasia of Miletus (see the Excursus in chapter 6). Aspasia was noted for her intellect and her expertise both in speaking and in matters of love. She was the famously honored companion of Athens' leading citizen

Pericles, whose popular nickname, as found in fragments of comic plays, was "Zeus." Ancient readers would not have missed the allusion of a name meaning "honored by Zeus" to Pericles' beloved Aspasia.

Socrates' report of Diotima's speech is followed by the abrupt entrance of the playboy-politician Alcibiades, who inserts himself in the space between Socrates and Agathon and proceeds to give the longest contribution of all to the debate. The discussion of Eros as a god, demigod, or force of nature, which characterized previous contributions, is abandoned. Instead, Plato has Alcibiades depict the person of Socrates himself as a mentor, hero, and the epitome of *erōs*. It is a brilliant and moving conclusion to this variegated and powerful philosophical exploration of the meaning of Love.

An Outline of the *Symposium*

A group of men gathers one evening for a party to celebrate the success of their host, the playwright Agathon. Two days earlier Agathon had won first prize at Athens' premiere dramatic festival with a tragic drama; we know that this was in 416 BCE, which is therefore the dialogue's "dramatic date" (the date the story is set). Agathon and his friends are hungover from drinking at the previous night's festivities, so they agree not to drink at this gathering, but to hold a speech competition instead. The topic suggested for the competition is the praise of Love.

As *erōs* is also the name of the god Eros, there is a constant equivocation throughout the speeches between praise of the god as a personal figure and the exploration of *erōs* as a notion. The powers and behaviors attributed to Eros can, for the most part, be easily understood as equivalent to the forces and qualities of love.

Plato tells the story of the evening through the mouth of someone who wasn't there (Apollodorus), repeating what he heard from someone (Glaucon) who had heard it from someone who was present (Aristodemus). This careful distancing of the story suggests that the *Symposium* should not be taken as a full or even true report of a real event. Instead, it should be recognized as a painstakingly crafted philosophical exploration of different perspectives on love. In the end, the dialogue constitutes an invitation to its readers to think for themselves about what *erōs* means, and about ways in which people may think and talk about love.

The dialogue falls into three sections:

Section I: The Five Speeches

The narrator Apollodorus first recounts how five diners took turns to give a speech in praise of Eros: the impetuous Phaedrus, the legalistic Pausanias, the physician Eryximachus, the comedian Aristophanes, and the tragedian Agathon. Each of these men gives their own partial view of what love can mean:

> The first speaker, Phaedrus, proposes that love is a source of inspiration to act nobly: the lover is even prepared to die for love.
>
> Pausanias makes a distinction between the "higher" form of true love and the "lower" form of sexual attraction, arguing for the importance of a lasting spiritual attachment between lover and beloved.

Eryximachus widens the scope of the question, speaking of love as an abstract, universal, harmonizing force in medicine, nature and music.

Aristophanes spins a comic fantasy to illustrate how and why love involves "searching for one's other half" to achieve a sense of fulfillment and joyful completion.

Agathon rounds off this section of speeches by invoking the beauty and creative power of love, and entertaining his hearers with a poetic eulogy of Eros in florid rhetorical style.

SECTION II: SOCRATES' SPEECH

After the five opening speeches, Socrates tells the company that, unlike the previous speakers, he proposes not to praise Eros but to tell "the truth about love." He says he learned the truth about love over the course of several meetings with a woman called Diotima. Diotima presented the doctrine that love is a mystery into which one must be initiated by an expert: love begins with physical attraction, but goes on to culminate with a vision of beauty that transcends the physical and ultimately leads to the divine realm (the modern term "Platonic love" derives from this doctrine). True love, Diotima proposes, is a relationship that draws out the enduring and creative qualities of the lover and the beloved. In the end, the complete lover may achieve the privilege of being admitted to an eternal, unchanging vision of love. This speech is the culmination of the speakers' philosophical and intellectual approaches to the topic of love that come across as largely abstract and impersonal.

SECTION III: ALCIBIADES' SPEECH

What follows Socrates' speech marks an abrupt change of register. The exuberant playboy-politician Alcibiades bursts in on the party in a state of drunken disarray. He delivers a speech praising the extraordinary and lovable personality of Socrates himself, the man who, he says, has always loved him and has elicited his fervent love in turn.

Just as Diotima's doctrine incorporated elements of the previous five speeches, Alcibiades' speech affirms and complements many aspects of those contributions. What Alcibiades proposes, however, is that, in talking about love, the particular relationship and the personalities of lover and beloved need to be taken into account, not just the abstraction of what love may mean.

A Note on the Translation and Ordering

Despite its appealing subject matter and generally conversational narrative, the *Symposium* is not an easy read. My aim has been to translate passages from the dialogue into English so that they remain as alive and natural as possible. The task is complicated by idiomatic structures in ancient Greek, such as the ubiquitous connective particles, and words and expressions that often have no direct equivalent in English. Plato was a master of Greek prose, and skillful at encompassing registers ranging from the casual and conversational to the rhetorically sophisticated and philosophically complex. If a translator attempts to be literal, the English often tends to sound contrived in a way the Greek does not. To convey the meaning both accurately and naturally, therefore, I have occasionally preferred to offer an accessible paraphrase in place of a word-for-word translation; and I have regularly ordered the prose into paragraphs to help readers grasp the units of thought.

The historical and cultural background of the dialogue requires compromises on the part of translator. *Erōs*, for example, the main term for love and desire (sexual and otherwise), is at the same time the name of the god Eros. The speakers use *erōs* in a way that keeps different connotations alive, but in English one must choose between "Eros," "Love," "love," "desire," and so on. Equally, the Greeks of Plato's time would readily have understood the distinction between *erastēs*, "lover," and *erōmenos*, "loved one"; the former was imagined as the older of the pair, the latter a boy (designated *paidika*, "boy-lover," where sex was involved). In English we might simply use "lover" for both sides of the relationship, but this does not differentiate the roles, while "boyfriend" or "sweetheart" are inappropriately romantic; so *erastēs* and *erōmenos* have been translated "lover" and "beloved."

For ease of cross-referencing the translations with the original Greek, I have divided the text of each of the passages into short sections to which letters are assigned. Where part of the text is omitted, this is shown by [-] placed after (and occasionally within or before) a passage of Greek text, and by [. . .] in the English text. A concordance to the standard numeration of the dialogue is given at the end.

HOW TO TALK ABOUT LOVE

Chapter 1

THE INSPIRER OF NOBLE DEEDS:
PHAEDRUS

Phaedrus has proposed the topic of praising love, more specifically the god Eros, to his fellow symposiasts. An idealistic young man, he starts off the first set of five speeches by arguing that Eros is the oldest of the gods and praiseworthy on that account. The Greeks honored old age, and the longevity of Eros implies that the god's blessings will be more numerous than those of younger gods. Phaedrus goes on to argue that love inspires lovers to aim for noble heights of action; he draws on a military image of heroism to commend those who risk their lives for the ones they love.

Citizens like Phaedrus were expected to fight in Athens' frequent battles against enemies such as Thebes and Sparta. Once enrolled as hoplites (heavy-armed infantrymen, who were required to supply their own suit of armor, shield, and weapons), they could be called up to go on campaign by land or sea. Many saw service on the battlefield as a chance to win glory as well as to fulfill their patriotic duty. Socrates himself, as we learn in the later part of the dialogue, was a courageous and effective hoplite soldier who participated in many battles on Athens' behalf.

What a lover wants, Phaedrus argues, is to win the respect and admiration of his beloved, and vice versa. An army composed of lovers would fight valiantly to preserve their honor in the eyes of those they love. Such a force would be unbeatable, because

Love would inspire them to avoid any taint of disgrace or cowardice. Phaedrus will have known about such a force that had recently been formed in Thebes, the "Sacred Band"; and since he extends the idea of a partnership of lovers to a whole state, he is also likely to have in mind the way Sparta's militaristic society was organized.

Phaedrus admits that such love can inspire women as well as men. Alcestis, for example, the mythical heroine portrayed in Euripides' drama *Alcestis*, was willing to lay down her life on behalf of her husband when no one else would, and as a result of her heroic conduct the gods allowed her to resume life among the living. Eros is praised by Phaedrus as the god who inspires such people to behave with nobility and makes them worthy of the greatest rewards.

Albeit in rather narrow terms, then, Phaedrus presents the idea of love as a force for good in human life, particularly when two individuals are strongly connected by a loving bond. This is a behavioral rather than psychological understanding of love; while honor and shame are involved, nothing is said about feelings such as intense affection or romantic passion. Many questions remain unanswered. How does love arise between two people in the first place? Since love sometimes leads to negative as well as positive behaviors, can it be presented unequivocally as a force for good? If love is thought of solely as inspiring success in battle and a willingness to make the ultimate sacrifice, where does this leave love's positive, creative, and life-enhancing dimensions? These and similar objections will be recognized in

some form and accounted for by subsequent
speakers in the dialogue.

Α. πρῶτον μὲν γάρ, ὥσπερ λέγω, ἔφη
Φαῖδρον ἀρξάμενον ἐνθένδε ποθὲν λέγειν,
ὅτι μέγας θεὸς εἴη ὁ Ἔρως καὶ θαυμαστὸς
ἐν ἀνθρώποις τε καὶ θεοῖς, πολλαχῇ μὲν
καὶ ἄλλῃ, οὐχ ἥκιστα δὲ κατὰ τὴν γένεσιν.
τὸ γὰρ ἐν τοῖς πρεσβύτατον εἶναι τὸν θεὸν
τίμιον, ἦ δ᾽ ὅς, τεκμήριον δὲ τούτου· γονῆς
γὰρ Ἔρωτος οὔτ᾽ εἰσὶν οὔτε λέγονται ὑπ᾽
οὐδενὸς οὔτε ἰδιώτου οὔτε ποιητοῦ, ἀλλ᾽
Ἡσίοδος πρῶτον μὲν Χάος φησὶ γενέσθαι

                αὐτὰρ ἔπειτα
Γαῖ᾽ εὐρύστερνος, πάντων ἕδος ἀσφαλὲς
   αἰεί,
   ἠδ᾽ Ἔρος

                    [*Theogony* 116]

Phaedrus: Translation and Text

A. Phaedrus began by saying something like this:

First of all, I say that Eros is revered among gods and men for lots of reasons, but not least because of his origins. He's the oldest of all the gods, as shown by the fact that he has no parents—no prose author or poet assigns any to him. Hesiod says that the first element to arise was Space,

> *And after that*
> *wide-breasted Earth, the world's secure,*
> *   eternal, base;*
> *then Love.*

Ἡσιόδῳ δὲ καὶ Ἀκουσίλεως σύμφησιν μετὰ τὸ Χάος δύο τούτω γενέσθαι, Γῆν τε καὶ Ἔρωτα. Παρμενίδης δὲ τὴν γένεσιν λέγει—

πρώτιστον μὲν Ἔρωτα θεῶν μητίσατο
πάντων.

οὕτω πολλαχόθεν ὁμολογεῖται ὁ Ἔρως ἐν τοῖς πρεσβύτατος εἶναι. πρεσβύτατος δὲ ὢν μεγίστων ἀγαθῶν ἡμῖν αἴτιός ἐστιν.

Β. οὐ γὰρ ἔγωγ᾽ ἔχω εἰπεῖν ὅτι μεῖζόν ἐστιν ἀγαθὸν εὐθὺς νέῳ ὄντι ἢ ἐραστὴς χρηστὸς καὶ ἐραστῇ παιδικά. ὃ γὰρ χρὴ ἀνθρώποις ἡγεῖσθαι παντὸς τοῦ βίου τοῖς μέλλουσι καλῶς βιώσεσθαι, τοῦτο οὔτε συγγένεια οἵα τε ἐμποιεῖν οὕτω καλῶς οὔτε τιμαὶ οὔτε πλοῦτος οὔτ᾽ ἄλλο οὐδὲν ὡς ἔρως. λέγω δὲ δὴ τί τοῦτο; τὴν ἐπὶ μὲν τοῖς αἰσχροῖς αἰσχύνην, ἐπὶ δὲ τοῖς καλοῖς φιλοτιμίαν· οὐ

Like Hesiod, Akousilaos says that after Space these two elements, Earth and Love, came into being. Parmenides also speaks of Love's birth, saying

> *The first of all the gods conceived was*
> *Love.*

Many sources attest, then, that Love is the most ancient of gods. On account of his longevity, he deserves thanks for providing the longest series of blessings to humankind.

B. Personally I can't think of a greater blessing than to have a praiseworthy lover in one's youth, or for a lover to have an admirable beloved. If we want to live fulfilling lives, what we need to guide us can't be attained from family connections, success, or wealth, or from anything more than love. Let me explain. People who do bad things bring shame on themselves, and those who

γὰρ ἔστιν ἄνευ τούτων οὔτε πόλιν οὔτε
ἰδιώτην μεγάλα καὶ καλὰ ἔργα ἐξεργάζεσθαι.

φημὶ τοίνυν ἐγὼ ἄνδρα ὅστις ἐρᾷ, εἴ τι
αἰσχρὸν ποιῶν κατάδηλος γίγνοιτο ἢ
πάσχων ὑπό του δι᾽ ἀνανδρίαν μὴ ἀμυνό-
μενος, οὔτ᾽ ἂν ὑπὸ πατρὸς ὀφθέντα οὕτως
ἀλγῆσαι οὔτε ὑπὸ ἑταίρων οὔτε ὑπ᾽ ἄλλου
οὐδενὸς ὡς ὑπὸ παιδικῶν. ταὐτὸν δὲ τοῦτο
καὶ τὸν ἐρώμενον ὁρῶμεν, ὅτι διαφερόντως τοὺς ἐραστὰς αἰσχύνεται, ὅταν ὀφθῇ
ἐν αἰσχρῷ τινι ὤν. εἰ οὖν μηχανή τις γένοιτο ὥστε πόλιν γενέσθαι ἢ στρατόπεδον
ἐραστῶν τε καὶ παιδικῶν, οὐκ ἔστιν ὅπως
ἂν ἄμεινον οἰκήσειαν τὴν ἑαυτῶν ἢ
ἀπεχόμενοι πάντων τῶν αἰσχρῶν καὶ
φιλοτιμούμενοι πρὸς ἀλλήλους, καὶ μαχό-
μενοί γ᾽ ἂν μετ᾽ ἀλλήλων οἱ τοιοῦτοι νικῷεν
ἂν ὀλίγοι ὄντες ὡς ἔπος εἰπεῖν πάντας
ἀνθρώπους.

act nobly gain renown. No city or individual who fails to respect these guidelines can accomplish anything honorable or good.

The fact is that lovers found doing something unworthy, or failing to stand up for themselves when abused, would be more bothered to be caught out by their beloveds than by their own fathers, friends, or anyone else. Similarly, if a beloved were observed doing something unworthy, he'd feel the same way vis-à-vis his lover. So if we could create cities or armies consisting of lovers and their beloveds, they'd be supremely successful, because they'd compete with each other to do good and would strain every sinew to avoid disgrace. Lovers paired off in this way and fighting shoulder to shoulder, even if they were few in number, could effectively conquer the world.

C. ἐρῶν γὰρ ἀνὴρ ὑπὸ παιδικῶν ὀφθῆναι
ἢ λιπὼν τάξιν ἢ ὅπλα ἀποβαλὼν ἧττον ἂν
δήπου δέξαιτο ἢ ὑπὸ πάντων τῶν ἄλλων, καὶ
πρὸ τούτου τεθνάναι ἂν πολλάκις ἕλοιτο. καὶ
μὴν ἐγκαταλιπεῖν γε τὰ παιδικὰ ἢ μὴ βοηθῆ-
σαι κινδυνεύοντι—οὐδεὶς οὕτω κακὸς
ὅντινα οὐκ ἂν αὐτὸς ὁ Ἔρως ἔνθεον ποιή-
σειε πρὸς ἀρετήν, ὥστε ὅμοιον εἶναι τῷ
ἀρίστῳ φύσει· καὶ ἀτεχνῶς, ὃ ἔφη Ὅμηρος,
"μένος ἐμπνεῦσαι" [*Iliad* 10.482, 15.262]
ἐνίοις τῶν ἡρώων τὸν θεόν, τοῦτο ὁ Ἔρως
τοῖς ἐρῶσι παρέχει γιγνόμενον παρ᾽ αὐτοῦ.
καὶ μὴν ὑπεραποθνήσκειν γε μόνοι ἐθέλου-
σιν οἱ ἐρῶντες, οὐ μόνον ὅτι ἄνδρες, ἀλλὰ
καὶ αἱ γυναῖκες.

τούτου δὲ καὶ ἡ Πελίου θυγάτηρ Ἄλκηστις
ἱκανὴν μαρτυρίαν παρέχεται ὑπὲρ τοῦδε τοῦ
λόγου εἰς τοὺς Ἕλληνας, ἐθελήσασα μόνη
ὑπὲρ τοῦ αὑτῆς ἀνδρὸς ἀποθανεῖν, ὄντων
αὐτῷ πατρός τε καὶ μητρός, οὓς ἐκείνη το-

C. If a lover abandoned his post or armor in battle, he'd clearly want the whole world to witness it rather than his beloved. He'd prefer to die a thousand deaths rather than let that happen. Who would desert or abandon someone he loves in their moment of danger? At that juncture the most arrant coward becomes the bravest of heroes, because Love itself inspires his courage. Homer says simply that the god "breathes spirit" into the souls of certain heroes; and that's what Love arouses and breathes into lovers. Love and love alone is what makes people lay down their lives for those they love, and that goes for women as well as men.

A shining example of this for the Greeks is Alcestis, daughter of Pelias, because she agreed, when no one else would, to give up her life for her husband. His father and mother might have taken the choice to do

σοῦτον ὑπερεβάλετο τῇ φιλίᾳ διὰ τὸν ἔρωτα,
ὥστε ἀποδεῖξαι αὐτοὺς ἀλλοτρίους ὄντας τῷ
ὑεῖ καὶ ὀνόματι μόνον προσήκοντας, καὶ
τοῦτ᾽ ἐργασαμένη τὸ ἔργον οὕτω καλὸν
ἔδοξεν ἐργάσασθαι οὐ μόνον ἀνθρώποις
ἀλλὰ καὶ θεοῖς, ὥστε πολλῶν πολλὰ καὶ καλὰ
ἐργασαμένων εὐαριθμήτοις δή τισιν ἔδοσαν
τοῦτο γέρας οἱ θεοί, ἐξ Ἅιδου ἀνεῖναι πάλιν
τὴν ψυχήν, ἀλλὰ τὴν ἐκείνης ἀνεῖσαν ἀγα-
σθέντες τῷ ἔργῳ· οὕτω καὶ θεοὶ τὴν περὶ τὸν
ἔρωτα σπουδήν τε καὶ ἀρετὴν μάλιστα
τιμῶσιν.

D. Ὀρφέα δὲ τὸν Οἰάγρου ἀτελῆ ἀπέπεμψαν ἐξ Ἅιδου, φάσμα δείξαντες τῆς γυναικὸς
ἐφ᾽ ἣν ἧκεν, αὐτὴν δὲ οὐ δόντες, ὅτι μαλθα-
κίζεσθαι ἐδόκει, ἅτε ὢν κιθαρῳδός, καὶ οὐ
τολμᾶν ἕνεκα τοῦ ἔρωτος ἀποθνῄσκειν
ὥσπερ Ἄλκηστις, ἀλλὰ διαμηχανᾶσθαι ζῶν
εἰσιέναι εἰς Ἅιδου.

so, but Alcestis' devotion, borne of love, was so much stronger than theirs that his parents might as well have been related to him in name only, not by blood. Her action was viewed as so heroic by gods no less than men that she, out of the many mortals famed for their deeds, is almost alone in having been allowed by the gods to come back alive from death. Such is the supreme honor the gods pay to loyalty and heroism when these qualities are inspired by love.

D. By contrast, the gods sent back Orpheus, Oeagrus's son, empty-handed from the Underworld. Instead of rewarding him by granting him the wife he'd descended to Hades to rescue, they gave him only the opportunity to see her ghost. In their eyes he was pusillanimous because, being a lyre-player, he, unlike Alcestis, hadn't risked

τοιγάρτοι διὰ ταῦτα δίκην αὐτῷ ἐπέθεσαν, καὶ ἐποίησαν τὸν θάνατον αὐτοῦ ὑπὸ γυναικῶν γενέσθαι, οὐχ ὥσπερ Ἀχιλλέα τὸν τῆς Θέτιδος ὑὸν ἐτίμησαν καὶ εἰς μακάρων νήσους ἀπέπεμψαν, ὅτι πεπυσμένος παρὰ τῆς μητρὸς ὡς ἀποθανοῖτο ἀποκτείνας Ἕκτορα, μὴ ποιήσας δὲ τοῦτο οἴκαδε ἐλθὼν γηραιὸς τελευτήσοι, ἐτόλμησεν ἑλέσθαι βοηθήσας τῷ ἐραστῇ Πατρόκλῳ καὶ τιμωρήσας οὐ μόνον ὑπεραποθανεῖν ἀλλὰ καὶ ἐπαποθανεῖν τετελευτηκότι· ὅθεν δὴ καὶ ὑπεραγασθέντες οἱ θεοὶ διαφερόντως αὐτὸν ἐτίμησαν, ὅτι τὸν ἐραστὴν οὕτω περὶ πολλοῦ ἐποιεῖτο.

Αἰσχύλος δὲ φλυαρεῖ φάσκων Ἀχιλλέα Πατρόκλου ἐρᾶν, ὃς ἦν καλλίων οὐ μόνον Πατρόκλου ἀλλ’ ἅμα καὶ τῶν ἡρώων ἁπάντων, καὶ ἔτι ἀγένειος, ἔπειτα νεώτερος πολύ, ὥς φησιν Ὅμηρος.

dying for love, but had contrived to enter the Underworld alive.

So the gods penalized Orpheus by making him die at the hands of women, and denying him the honor granted to Thetis's son Achilles, who was sent to the Isles of the Blest because he'd made the heroic choice. His mother had told him that if he killed Hector he would die, and that, if he didn't, he would return home and live to happy old age. So when Achilles entered the fray to avenge his lover Patroclus, he made the choice not only to risk dying, but actually to die, by fighting on his behalf. The gods were particularly touched, and honored Achilles especially highly because he accorded such regard to his older lover.

Apropos of which, Aeschylus is talking nonsense when he makes Achilles Patroclus's lover rather than vice versa. Achilles

Ε. ἀλλὰ γὰρ τῷ ὄντι μάλιστα μὲν ταύτην
τὴν ἀρετὴν οἱ θεοὶ τιμῶσιν τὴν περὶ τὸν
ἔρωτα, μᾶλλον μέντοι θαυμάζουσιν καὶ
ἄγανται καὶ εὖ ποιοῦσιν ὅταν ὁ ἐρώμενος
τὸν ἐραστὴν ἀγαπᾷ, ἢ ὅταν ὁ ἐραστὴς τὰ
παιδικά. θειότερον γὰρ ἐραστὴς παιδικῶν·
ἔνθεος γάρ ἐστι. διὰ ταῦτα καὶ τὸν Ἀχιλλέα
τῆς Ἀλκήστιδος μᾶλλον ἐτίμησαν, εἰς
μακάρων νήσους ἀποπέμψαντες.

οὕτω δὴ ἔγωγέ φημι Ἔρωτα θεῶν καὶ
πρεσβύτατον καὶ τιμιώτατον καὶ κυριώτατον
εἶναι εἰς ἀρετῆς καὶ εὐδαιμονίας κτῆσιν
ἀνθρώποις καὶ ζῶσι καὶ τελευτήσασιν.

was more handsome than all the heroes, including Patroclus, and the fact that he's portrayed as beardless in Homer means he's much younger than Patroclus.

E. Anyway, it's clear that the gods have the highest regard for the heroism that arises from love, and are even more admiring and generous when it's the younger beloved who cherishes the older lover rather than vice versa. The lover, you see, is closer to the gods than the younger man is, because Love has already entered into him. So for all these reasons the gods rewarded Achilles even more highly than they did Alcestis, and sent him to the Isles of the Blest.

To sum up, my claim is that Eros is the most ancient and respected of the gods, and that Love is the supreme force that helps human beings to attain the highest and most desirable goals, both in life and in death.

Chapter 2

A VIRTUOUS AND LASTING UNION: *PAUSANIAS*

After a few more speeches that are omitted by the narrator because he can't remember them, Pausanias, the lover of the party's young host Agathon, follows Phaedrus with a long and somewhat repetitive speech that reflects his fervor for the kind of relationship in which he himself is involved. He starts by taking issue with Phaedrus's premise that the symposiasts should speak simply "in praise" of Love. Pausanias insists that not all kinds of love are praiseworthy, and he seeks to draw a distinction between proper and improper expressions of love.

Pausanias adopts a legalistic attitude in defending the Athenian custom (Greek *nomos* means both "custom" and "law") that allows for the love of older men for younger boys. While this practice was a recognized feature of upper-class Athenian life, the sexual partnerships to which it led aroused disapproval and disquiet in many quarters (not least the fathers of the young boys concerned) and were even forbidden and legally sanctioned in other Greek cities.

The activities that Greeks associated with excellence and glory, such as warfare, athletics, and rhetoric, were exclusively male domains. Athenian girls had no education or athletic training, and to ensure their suitability for marriage they were often wedded or betrothed in their early teens. Women could not, therefore, be expected to act as intellectual or spiritual companions to Athenian men, who sought other outlets for their sexual desires and social pleasures, including the companionship of younger men and boys. Such partnerships could in turn help younger men develop their intellectual resources and improve their social opportunities; Socrates himself is reported to have had in his teens an amorous relationship with an older philosopher, Archelaus. But the possibility that boys might be used or abused purely for sexual gratification was an ever-present reproach, and one that Pausanias seeks to counter. He wants to insist that true love should be honorable, involving mutuality and consent, and further argues for this principle to be enshrined in law. He invokes a strong duality between honorable and dishonorable kinds of love.

To illustrate his point, Pausanias draws on two different versions of the myth of the birth of Aphrodite, the goddess of love and inseparable companion of Eros. Whereas in

Hesiod's *Theogony* Aphrodite is identified as the daughter of Ouranos (Heaven) and no mother is assigned to her, in Homer's *Iliad* she is said to be the daughter of Zeus and Dione. Pausanias therefore posits the existence of two separate goddesses: to the former goddess he assigns the epithet "Heavenly" (Uranian), while the latter he calls "Popular." The alleged birth of Uranian Aphrodite from a male parent alone prompts him to allege that relations between men are less primarily sexual in nature, and therefore more honorable, than are relations between men and women.

Pausanias argues that it is the duty of an older, wiser male partner, a devotee of "heavenly" *erōs*, to provide intellectual and other benefits to a younger one, and to make a faithful and lasting commitment that aims at the younger man's improvement and education. Later in the dialogue, Plato will present the scenario of the younger Alcibiades attempting and failing to seduce the older Socrates. The latter's apparent obliviousness to Alcibiades' physical charms, and his acknowledged wish to do nothing other than improve his protégé's soul, instantiates the "good" love Pausanias espouses.

The modern reader, however, will baulk at Pausanias's generalizations about the more overtly sexual nature of heterosexual love, the disparity between men and women, and the alleged benefits of an intimate relationship between a man and boy. But Pausanias's speech fills a gap in Phaedrus's account, which lacked an explanation of how love may arise in the first place and how it operates within loving couples. Here there is a frank acknowledgment that sex and physical attraction play a key role. That creates an imperative for human beings to consider how best to regulate their desires. Pausanias recognizes that sexual desire, once satisfied, may easily be transferred to a new object, leaving anger and distress in its wake. So how, he asks, can negative consequences be avoided?

Pausanias's answer is a strong espousal of fidelity and commitment; steady relationships and quasi-marital stability are, for him, the signs of true and noble love. And while his distinction between love driven by sexual desire and love undertaken with noble intentions might appear overly simple and idealistic, it paves the way for the message in Socrates' speech—that while love may begin with physical attraction, in its highest manifestation it will transcend the physical and attain to the spiritual.

Α. οὐ καλῶς μοι δοκεῖ, ὦ Φαῖδρε, προβε-
βλῆσθαι ἡμῖν ὁ λόγος, τὸ ἁπλῶς οὕτως
παρηγγέλθαι ἐγκωμιάζειν Ἔρωτα. εἰ μὲν
γὰρ εἷς ἦν ὁ Ἔρως, καλῶς ἂν εἶχε, νῦν δὲ οὐ
γάρ ἐστιν εἷς· μὴ ὄντος δὲ ἑνὸς ὀρθότερόν
ἐστι πρότερον προρρηθῆναι ὁποῖον δεῖ
ἐπαινεῖν. ἐγὼ οὖν πειράσομαι τοῦτο ἐπανορ-
θώσασθαι, πρῶτον μὲν Ἔρωτα φράσαι ὃν
δεῖ ἐπαινεῖν, ἔπειτα ἐπαινέσαι ἀξίως τοῦ
θεοῦ.

Β. πάντες γὰρ ἴσμεν ὅτι οὐκ ἔστιν ἄνευ
Ἔρωτος Ἀφροδίτη. μιᾶς μὲν οὖν οὔσης εἷς
ἂν ἦν Ἔρως· ἐπεὶ δὲ δὴ δύο ἐστόν, δύο
ἀνάγκη καὶ Ἔρωτε εἶναι. πῶς δ᾽ οὐ δύο τὼ

Pausanias: Translation and Text

A. I think the scope of our discussion has been unhelpfully defined, Phaedrus, because we've been instructed simply to praise Love. If Love were a single god, that would be fine, but the fact is that there's more than one Eros. So we should first decide which Eros is to be praised. I'll try to amend this by first identifying which of the Loves merits praise, then I'll praise that god in the manner he deserves.

B. We all know that Aphrodite and Eros go hand in hand. Now, if there were only one Aphrodite, there would be only one Eros; but, in fact, there are two Aphrodites, so there must also be two separate Eroses. It's clear enough that there are two goddesses, right? There's the older one,

θεά; ἡ μέν γέ που πρεσβυτέρα καὶ ἀμήτωρ
Οὐρανοῦ θυγάτηρ, ἣν δὴ καὶ Οὐρανίαν
ἐπονομάζομεν· ἡ δὲ νεωτέρα Διὸς καὶ
Διώνης, ἣν δὴ Πάνδημον καλοῦμεν. ἀναγκαῖον δὴ καὶ Ἔρωτα τὸν μὲν τῇ ἑτέρᾳ
συνεργὸν Πάνδημον ὀρθῶς καλεῖσθαι, τὸν
δὲ Οὐράνιον.

C. ἐπαινεῖν μὲν οὖν δεῖ πάντας θεούς, ἃ δ᾽
οὖν ἑκάτερος εἴληχε πειρατέον εἰπεῖν. πᾶσα
γὰρ πρᾶξις ὧδ᾽ ἔχει· αὐτὴ ἐφ᾽ ἑαυτῆς
πραττομένη οὔτε καλὴ οὔτε αἰσχρά. οἷον
ὃ νῦν ἡμεῖς ποιοῦμεν, ἢ πίνειν ἢ ᾄδειν ἢ
διαλέγεσθαι, οὐκ ἔστι τούτων αὐτὸ καλὸν
οὐδέν, ἀλλ᾽ ἐν τῇ πράξει, ὡς ἂν πραχθῇ,
τοιοῦτον ἀπέβη· καλῶς μὲν γὰρ πραττόμε-
νον καὶ ὀρθῶς καλὸν γίγνεται, μὴ ὀρθῶς
δὲ αἰσχρόν. οὕτω δὴ καὶ τὸ ἐρᾶν καὶ ὁ
Ἔρως οὐ πᾶς ἐστι καλὸς οὐδὲ ἄξιος
ἐγκωμιάζεσθαι, ἀλλὰ ὁ καλῶς προτρέπων
ἐρᾶν.

born of Ouranos without a mother, who we call "Heavenly" Aphrodite, and the younger one, the daughter of Zeus and Dione, who we call "Popular" Aphrodite. It follows that the Eros who's linked to the latter should be called "Popular Love" and the other one "Heavenly Love."

C. While it's a requirement that all gods be praised, we should seek to distinguish the different domains of the two Loves. In fact, this holds for everything we do, since no action is good or bad in itself. Take what we're doing now, drinking, singing, and debating—none of these actions is good in itself. The judgment of worth depends on the particular action, and on the way it's performed. If it's done in a decent and proper way, it's good; if not, it's bad. This is the case with love and with Eros. Not all kinds of love are good and praiseworthy,

D. Ὁ μὲν οὖν τῆς Πανδήμου Ἀφροδίτης ὡς ἀληθῶς πάνδημός ἐστι καὶ ἐξεργάζεται ὅτι ἂν τύχῃ· καὶ οὗτός ἐστιν ὃν οἱ φαῦλοι τῶν ἀνθρώπων ἐρῶσιν. ἐρῶσι δὲ οἱ τοιοῦτοι πρῶτον μὲν οὐχ ἧττον γυναικῶν ἢ παίδων, ἔπειτα ὧν καὶ ἐρῶσι τῶν σωμάτων μᾶλλον ἢ τῶν ψυχῶν, ἔπειτα ὡς ἂν δύνωνται ἀνοητοτάτων, πρὸς τὸ διαπράξασθαι μόνον βλέποντες, ἀμελοῦντες δὲ τοῦ καλῶς ἢ μή· ὅθεν δὴ συμβαίνει αὐτοῖς ὅτι ἂν τύχωσι τοῦτο πράττειν, ὁμοίως μὲν ἀγαθόν, ὁμοίως δὲ τοὐναντίον.

ἔστι γὰρ καὶ ἀπὸ τῆς θεοῦ νεωτέρας τε οὔσης πολὺ ἢ τῆς ἑτέρας, καὶ μετεχούσης ἐν τῇ γενέσει καὶ θήλεος καὶ ἄρρενος. ὁ δὲ τῆς Οὐρανίας πρῶτον μὲν οὐ μετεχούσης θή-

only the kind that encourages us to love in a proper way.

D. The Eros that's linked to Popular Aphrodite is vulgar and undiscriminating—the kind of love that common people go in for. Such people are apt to love women as well as boys, and will love people for their bodies rather than their souls. They chase after folk who are as dull as can be, because all they want is to get their way with them, and they don't care about what's right or wrong. In the end, whether the outcome is positive or negative, their conduct is undiscriminating. This sort of love is associated with the much younger of the two goddesses, the one born from both female and male. The Eros who accompanies the Heavenly goddess, however, and who has no female parent but only a male one, inspires love for boys. As

λεος ἀλλ᾽ ἄρρενος μόνον—καὶ ἔστιν οὗτος ὁ
τῶν παίδων ἔρως—ἔπειτα πρεσβυτέρας,
ὕβρεως ἀμοίρου· ὅθεν δὴ ἐπὶ τὸ ἄρρεν
τρέπονται οἱ ἐκ τούτου τοῦ ἔρωτος ἔπιπνοι,
τὸ φύσει ἐρρωμενέστερον καὶ νοῦν μᾶλλον
ἔχον ἀγαπῶντες.

E. καί τις ἂν γνοίη καὶ ἐν αὐτῇ τῇ παιδε-
ραστίᾳ τοὺς εἰλικρινῶς ὑπὸ τούτου τοῦ
ἔρωτος ὡρμημένους· οὐ γὰρ ἐρῶσι παίδων,
ἀλλ᾽ ἐπειδὰν ἤδη ἄρχωνται νοῦν ἴσχειν,
τοῦτο δὲ πλησιάζει τῷ γενειάσκειν. παρε-
σκευασμένοι γὰρ οἶμαί εἰσιν οἱ ἐντεῦθεν
ἀρχόμενοι ἐρᾶν ὡς τὸν βίον ἅπαντα συνεσό-
μενοι καὶ κοινῇ συμβιωσόμενοι, ἀλλ᾽ οὐκ
ἐξαπατήσαντες, ἐν ἀφροσύνῃ λαβόντες ὡς
νέον, καταγελάσαντες οἰχήσεσθαι ἐπ᾽ ἄλλον
ἀποτρέχοντες. [-]

the older of the two goddesses, Heavenly Aphrodite commits none of the abuses that characterize her counterpart. Those inspired by her love turn to male lovers, because they're attracted to people who are naturally strong and intelligent.

E. One can recognize the people who are inspired purely by this kind of *erōs*. The purity of their pursuit is manifest in the fact that it's not children they love, but only boys whose minds are beginning to develop, those who are at the stage when their beard starts to show. I find that those who choose boys of that age as their companions generally commit themselves to lifelong relationships and to sharing their lives with their partners, rather than just taking advantage of the inexperience of their boyfriends and then humiliating them by running off after some other object of desire. [. . .]

F. αἰσχρῶς μὲν οὖν ἐστι πονηρῷ τε καὶ πονηρῶς χαρίζεσθαι, καλῶς δὲ χρηστῷ τε καὶ καλῶς. πονηρὸς δ᾽ ἐστὶν ἐκεῖνος ὁ ἐραστὴς ὁ πάνδημος, ὁ τοῦ σώματος μᾶλλον ἢ τῆς ψυχῆς ἐρῶν· καὶ γὰρ οὐδὲ μόνιμός ἐστιν, ἅτε οὐδὲ μονίμου ἐρῶν πράγματος. ἅμα γὰρ τῷ τοῦ σώματος ἄνθει λήγοντι, οὗπερ ἤρα, "οἴχεται ἀποπτάμενος," πολλοὺς λόγους καὶ ὑποσχέσεις καταισχύνας· ὁ δὲ τοῦ ἤθους χρηστοῦ ὄντος ἐραστὴς διὰ βίου μένει, ἅτε μονίμῳ συντακείς. [-]

G. νενόμισται γὰρ δὴ ἡμῖν, ἐάν τις ἐθέλῃ τινὰ θεραπεύειν ἡγούμενος δι᾽ ἐκεῖνον ἀμείνων ἔσεσθαι ἢ κατὰ σοφίαν τινὰ ἢ κατὰ ἄλλο ὁτιοῦν μέρος ἀρετῆς, αὕτη αὖ ἡ ἐθελο-δουλεία οὐκ αἰσχρὰ εἶναι οὐδὲ κολακεία. δεῖ δὴ τὼ νόμω τούτω συμβαλεῖν εἰς ταὐτόν,

F. It's wrong to grant improper sexual favors to an unprincipled person, but not to grant proper favors to a good person. The common lover who loves the body more than the soul is not only unprincipled but inconstant, since he's not in love with anything that will last. When the attractive qualities of the body that initially aroused his desire wear off, he "takes to his heels," flouting repeated assurances and breaking his promises. A lover of someone's fine character, by contrast, lasts for a lifetime, because he's attached himself to something that is itself of enduring worth. [...]

G. It's generally agreed that if one renders willing service to a person who improves one intellectually or in some other way, it shouldn't be regarded as shameful or ingratiating behavior. Two laws come into play if a boy is to be allowed to encourage a

τόν τε περὶ τὴν παιδεραστίαν καὶ τὸν περὶ
τὴν φιλοσοφίαν τε καὶ τὴν ἄλλην ἀρετήν, εἰ
μέλλει συμβῆναι καλὸν γενέσθαι τὸ ἐραστῇ
παιδικὰ χαρίσασθαι.

ὅταν γὰρ εἰς τὸ αὐτὸ ἔλθωσιν ἐραστής τε
καὶ παιδικά, νόμον ἔχων ἑκάτερος, ὁ μὲν
χαρισαμένοις παιδικοῖς ὑπηρετῶν ὁτιοῦν
δικαίως ἂν ὑπηρετεῖν, ὁ δὲ τῷ ποιοῦντι αὐτὸν
σοφόν τε καὶ ἀγαθὸν δικαίως αὖ ὁτιοῦν ἂν
ὑπουργῶν ὑπουργεῖν, καὶ ὁ μὲν δυνάμενος
εἰς φρόνησιν καὶ τὴν ἄλλην ἀρετὴν συμβάλ-
λεσθαι, ὁ δὲ δεόμενος εἰς παίδευσιν καὶ τὴν
ἄλλην σοφίαν κτᾶσθαι, τότε δὴ τούτων
συνιόντων εἰς ταὐτὸν τῶν νόμων μοναχοῦ
ἐνταῦθα συμπίπτει τὸ καλὸν εἶναι παιδικὰ
ἐραστῇ χαρίσασθαι, ἄλλοθι δὲ οὐδαμοῦ. [-]

Η. οὕτω πᾶν πάντως γε καλὸν ἀρετῆς γ'
ἕνεκα χαρίζεσθαι. οὗτός ἐστιν ὁ τῆς οὐρανίας
θεοῦ ἔρως καὶ οὐράνιος καὶ πολλοῦ ἄξιος

lover: one law concerns the love of boys, the other concerns the pursuit of wisdom and other kinds of excellence. [. . .]

When lover and beloved come together, each subject to these laws, the lover is entitled to help in any way the boy who gratifies him, while the beloved will rightly reciprocate the attentions of the lover who's concerned for his moral and intellectual improvement. Since the lover has wisdom and excellence to offer, while the beloved seeks education and knowledge generally, when these laws are brought into harmony, it's honorable for the boy to yield to the lover, but not under any other conditions. [. . .]

H. In sum, it's fine to grant any favor so long as what's being pursued is excellence. This is the kind of love that we

καὶ πόλει καὶ ἰδιώταις, πολλὴν ἐπιμέλειαν
ἀναγκάζων ποιεῖσθαι πρὸς ἀρετὴν τόν
τε ἐρῶντα αὐτὸν αὑτοῦ καὶ τὸν ἐρώμενον·
οἱ δ᾽ ἕτεροι πάντες τῆς ἑτέρας, τῆς
πανδήμου. [-]

attribute to the Heavenly Aphrodite. Not only is it divine, it's of great value to both state and individual, since it makes both lover and beloved attend to their own moral development. [...] All other kinds of love are the domain of the other goddess, Popular Aphrodite.

Chapter 3

A UNIVERSAL PRINCIPLE OF HARMONY: *ERYXIMACHUS*

After Pausanias, it is Aristophanes' turn to speak, but the comic poet is stricken by an attack of hiccups, so Eryximachus speaks first, allowing a largely abstract understanding of love to be introduced before Aristophanes spins his more earthy comic fantasy. Eryximachus presents the idea that love should not be limited to human interactions: it extends to everything in the world. He portrays love as a universal force that connects and harmonizes all beings and elements. Love is not just about romantic or interpersonal relationships, but may be seen to operate in the sphere of medicine, of music, and in the whole of nature.

Eryximachus builds on the distinction Pausanias has made between good and bad love. A doctor by profession, he proposes that medicine is the art of knowing how to satisfy healthy desires and to reject unhealthy ones, and how to reconcile both kinds of desire in the human body. Medicine seeks to harmonize opposing corporeal elements—the hot and the cold, wet and dry, bitter and sweet—just as music reconciles opposites in its own sphere: high and low pitches, short and long durations in rhythm. The contrasting seasons of the year and the circling movement of stars show how the universe as a whole exhibits the operation of love as a balance of different elements. For Eryximachus, love is the cosmic force that creates harmony in every realm of its operation.

Where previous speakers have described love in terms of human aims and behaviors, Eryximachus turns toward abstraction. Phaedrus has argued that Love is a force for good in lovers' aims and actions: Eryximachus builds on that idea by extending love's reconciling goodness to the universe as a whole. The duality posited by Pausanias is recognized, but the emphasis is on love's unifying power. Eryximachus's notion of love as a harmonizing force draws on the doctrine of Empedocles, a famous thinker of the early fifth century BCE who identified Love as the force that unites fundamental elements of the universe and brings about creation, competing with Strife, which dissolves and separates them. For Eryximachus, similarly, love is what brings together not just lovers, but everything that might benefit from being reconciled or harmonized—

bodily humors, musical notes, nature's pre-
cipitations, and the motion of stars. Tran-
scending individual desires and relationships,
Eros in this vision becomes a universal,
transformative, and unifying power.

Α. τὸ μὲν γὰρ διπλοῦν εἶναι τὸν Ἔρωτα
δοκεῖ μοι καλῶς διελέσθαι· ὅτι δὲ οὐ μόνον
ἐστὶν ἐπὶ ταῖς ψυχαῖς τῶν ἀνθρώπων πρὸς
τοὺς καλοὺς ἀλλὰ καὶ πρὸς ἄλλα πολλὰ καὶ
ἐν τοῖς ἄλλοις, τοῖς τε σώμασι τῶν πάντων
ζῴων καὶ τοῖς ἐν τῇ γῇ φυομένοις καὶ ὡς
ἔπος εἰπεῖν ἐν πᾶσι τοῖς οὖσι, καθεωρακέναι
μοι δοκῶ ἐκ τῆς ἰατρικῆς, τῆς ἡμετέρας
τέχνης, ὡς μέγας καὶ θαυμαστὸς καὶ ἐπὶ πᾶν
ὁ θεὸς τείνει καὶ κατ᾽ ἀνθρώπινα καὶ κατὰ
θεῖα πράγματα.

Β. ἄρξομαι δὲ ἀπὸ τῆς ἰατρικῆς λέγων, ἵνα
καὶ πρεσβεύωμεν τὴν τέχνην. ἡ γὰρ φύσις
τῶν σωμάτων τὸν διπλοῦν Ἔρωτα τοῦτον
ἔχει· τὸ γὰρ ὑγιὲς τοῦ σώματος καὶ τὸ
νοσοῦν ὁμολογουμένως ἕτερόν τε καὶ
ἀνόμοιόν ἐστι, τὸ δὲ ἀνόμοιον ἀνομοίων

Eryximachus: Translation and Text

A. I think the notion that Love has a two-fold aspect is a good distinction to make. But I also think this can be seen not only in the way human beings fall in love with people they find beautiful, but also in animals and plants and essentially all beings. This I observe from my own work as a doctor, which gives me an insight into how great and marvelous Love is, and how its divine force extends to everything on earth and in heaven.

B. To give my profession due honor, I'll start by speaking about medicine. Our bodily nature demonstrates Love's duality in the following way. The healthy element in the body is clearly separate and distinct from the sick one; and because these elements

ἐπιθυμεῖ καὶ ἐρᾷ. ἄλλος μὲν οὖν ὁ ἐπὶ τῷ
ὑγιεινῷ ἔρως, ἄλλος δὲ ὁ ἐπὶ τῷ νοσώδει.
ἔστιν δή, ὥσπερ ἄρτι Παυσανίας ἔλεγεν τοῖς
μὲν ἀγαθοῖς καλὸν χαρίζεσθαι τῶν ἀνθρώπων, τοῖς δ' ἀκολάστοις αἰσχρόν, οὕτω καὶ
ἐν αὐτοῖς τοῖς σώμασιν τοῖς μὲν ἀγαθοῖς
ἑκάστου τοῦ σώματος καὶ ὑγιεινοῖς καλὸν
χαρίζεσθαι καὶ δεῖ, καὶ τοῦτό ἐστιν ᾧ ὄνομα
τὸ ἰατρικόν, τοῖς δὲ κακοῖς καὶ νοσώδεσιν
αἰσχρόν τε καὶ δεῖ ἀχαριστεῖν, εἰ μέλλει τις
τεχνικὸς εἶναι.

C. ἔστι γὰρ ἰατρική, ὡς ἐν κεφαλαίῳ
εἰπεῖν, ἐπιστήμη τῶν τοῦ σώματος ἐρωτικῶν
πρὸς πλησμονὴν καὶ κένωσιν, καὶ ὁ διαγι-
γνώσκων ἐν τούτοις τὸν καλόν τε καὶ αἰσχρὸν ἔρωτα, οὗτός ἐστιν ὁ ἰατρικώτατος,
καὶ ὁ μεταβάλλειν ποιῶν, ὥστε ἀντὶ τοῦ
ἑτέρου ἔρωτος τὸν ἕτερον κτᾶσθαι, καὶ οἷς μὴ
ἔνεστιν ἔρως, δεῖ δ' ἐγγενέσθαι, ἐπιστάμενος
ἐμποιῆσαι καὶ ἐνόντα ἐξελεῖν, ἀγαθὸς ἂν εἴη

differ, what they crave and desire are different. In other words, desire means one thing for the healthy part of the body, and another for the sick part. Pausanias was saying just now that it's fine to encourage the desire of a good man but not to indulge an immoral one. So it is with the body; good, healthy elements should be encouraged—that's what's called the art of medicine—and sick, diseased parts should be discouraged. This is how a good doctor works.

C. Medicine may be summed up as the knowledge of the principles of desire in the body, and how best to satisfy or deny them. The best doctor is one who can distinguish good desires from bad, and who can convert one into the other. To be able to generate desire where it's needed, and to implant it or remove it, is what makes for a truly skilled practitioner. He must reconcile the most

δημιουργός. δεῖ γὰρ δὴ τὰ ἔχθιστα ὄντα ἐν
τῷ σώματι φίλα οἷόν τ᾽ εἶναι ποιεῖν καὶ ἐρᾶν
ἀλλήλων. ἔστι δὲ ἔχθιστα τὰ ἐναντιώτατα,
ψυχρὸν θερμῷ, πικρὸν γλυκεῖ, ξηρὸν ὑγρῷ,
πάντα τὰ τοιαῦτα· τούτοις ἐπιστηθεὶς ἔρωτα
ἐμποιῆσαι καὶ ὁμόνοιαν ὁ ἡμέτερος πρόγονος
Ἀσκληπιός, ὥς φασιν οἵδε οἱ ποιηταὶ καὶ ἐγὼ
πείθομαι, συνέστησεν τὴν ἡμετέραν τέχνην. ἥ
τε οὖν ἰατρική, ὥσπερ λέγω, πᾶσα διὰ τοῦ
θεοῦ τούτου κυβερνᾶται, ὡσαύτως δὲ καὶ
γυμναστικὴ καὶ γεωργία.

D. μουσικὴ δὲ καὶ παντὶ κατάδηλος τῷ καὶ
σμικρὸν προσέχοντι τὸν νοῦν ὅτι κατὰ ταὐτὰ
ἔχει τούτοις, ὥσπερ ἴσως καὶ Ἡράκλειτος
βούλεται λέγειν, ἐπεὶ τοῖς γε ῥήμασιν οὐ
καλῶς λέγει. τὸ ἓν γάρ φησι "διαφερόμενον
αὐτὸ αὑτῷ συμφέρεσθαι ὥσπερ ἁρμονίαν
τόξου τε καὶ λύρας." ἔστι δὲ πολλὴ ἀλογία
ἁρμονίαν φάναι διαφέρεσθαι ἢ ἐκ διαφερομένων ἔτι εἶναι. ἀλλὰ ἴσως τόδε ἐβούλετο

hostile elements in the body so that they learn to love each other. These are the elements that are most opposed to each other, such as cold and hot, bitter and sweet, dry and wet, and so on. I believe what the poets say about my ancestor Asclepius knowing how to implant love and harmony in these elements; that was how he established our profession. Every branch of the healing art is under the direction of the god, and it's the same thing with gymnastics and farming.

D. Music too, if you think about it, clearly exhibits the principle of the reconciliation of opposites, which is perhaps what Heraclitus means, though he phrases it obscurely, when says that a unity "in tension with itself is in harmony . . . as with the harmony of a bow or lyre." It's paradoxical to say that a harmony "is in tension," or that when elements are pulling in different directions

λέγειν, ὅτι ἐκ διαφερομένων πρότερον τοῦ
ὀξέος καὶ βαρέος, ἔπειτα ὕστερον ὁμολογησάντων γέγονεν ὑπὸ τῆς μουσικῆς τέχνης.
οὐ γὰρ δήπου ἐκ διαφερομένων γε ἔτι τοῦ
ὀξέος καὶ βαρέος ἁρμονία ἂν εἴη· ἡ γὰρ
ἁρμονία συμφωνία ἐστίν, συμφωνία δὲ
ὁμολογία τις—ὁμολογίαν δὲ ἐκ διαφερομένων, ἕως ἂν διαφέρωνται, ἀδύνατον εἶναι·
διαφερόμενον δὲ αὖ καὶ μὴ ὁμολογοῦν
ἀδύνατον ἁρμόσαι—ὥσπερ γε καὶ ὁ ῥυθμὸς
ἐκ τοῦ ταχέος καὶ βραδέος, ἐκ διενηνεγμέ-
νων πρότερον, ὕστερον δὲ ὁμολογησάντων
γέγονε.

E. τὴν δὲ ὁμολογίαν πᾶσι τούτοις, ὥσπερ
ἐκεῖ ἡ ἰατρική, ἐνταῦθα ἡ μουσικὴ ἐντίθησιν,
ἔρωτα καὶ ὁμόνοιαν ἀλλήλων ἐμποιήσασα·
καὶ ἔστιν αὖ μουσικὴ περὶ ἁρμονίαν καὶ
ῥυθμὸν ἐρωτικῶν ἐπιστήμη. καὶ ἐν μέν γε
αὐτῇ τῇ συστάσει ἁρμονίας τε καὶ ῥυθμοῦ

harmony still exists. But evidently what he was getting at was that high-pitched and low-pitched notes, though formally at odds with each other, are reconciled in the art of music, since there can be no harmony of high and low notes if they remain at odds. Harmony is concordance, and concordance is agreement; but there's no agreement if elements are still in disagreement, and there can be no harmony if elements are at odds and not in agreement. On a similar principle, rhythm is created by fast and slow elements that, though formally at odds with each other, are in practice brought into accord.

E. Just as we saw with medicine, then, music engenders accord in all these elements, bringing love and unanimity to them. So the art of music, too, is the understanding of the principles of love as applied to harmony and rhythm. There's no problem distinguishing

οὐδὲν χαλεπὸν τὰ ἐρωτικὰ διαγιγνώσκειν,
οὐδὲ ὁ διπλοῦς ἔρως ἐνταῦθά πω ἔστιν·
ἀλλ᾽ ἐπειδὰν δέῃ πρὸς τοὺς ἀνθρώπους
καταχρῆσθαι ῥυθμῷ τε καὶ ἁρμονίᾳ ἢ ποιοῦ-
ντα, ὃ δὴ μελοποιίαν καλοῦσιν, ἢ χρώμενον
ὀρθῶς τοῖς πεποιημένοις μέλεσί τε καὶ
μέτροις, ὃ δὴ παιδεία ἐκλήθη, ἐνταῦθα δὴ
καὶ χαλεπὸν καὶ ἀγαθοῦ δημιουργοῦ δεῖ.
    F. πάλιν γὰρ ἥκει ὁ αὐτὸς λόγος, ὅτι τοῖς
μὲν κοσμίοις τῶν ἀνθρώπων, καὶ ὡς ἂν
κοσμιώτεροι γίγνοιντο οἱ μήπω ὄντες, δεῖ
χαρίζεσθαι καὶ φυλάττειν τὸν τούτων
ἔρωτα, καὶ οὗτός ἐστιν ὁ καλός, ὁ οὐράνιος, ὁ τῆς Οὐρανίας μούσης Ἔρως· ὁ δὲ
Πολυμνίας ὁ πάνδημος, ὃν δεῖ εὐλαβούμε-
νον προσφέρειν οἷς ἂν προσφέρῃ, ὅπως ἂν
τὴν μὲν ἡδονὴν αὐτοῦ καρπώσηται, ἀκολα-
σίαν δὲ μηδεμίαν ἐμποιήσῃ, ὥσπερ ἐν τῇ
ἡμετέρᾳ τέχνῃ μέγα ἔργον ταῖς περὶ τὴν

good love from bad in the structures of harmony and rhythm—twofold love doesn't exist there. But when we present rhythm and harmony in practice, either when we write music for compositions or when we correctly perform those compositions as trained musicians, the task is challenging and a skilled practitioner is required.

F. What was said earlier applies here. It's right to offer one's services to people who behave with due discipline, and one should safeguard this kind of love in order to encourage others who haven't achieved that discipline to improve. This is the good love, Heavenly Love, which comes from the heavenly Muse. Meanwhile popular love is the realm of Polyhymnia, and one should apply it carefully, so that the pleasure she brings does not lead to indiscipline. Similarly, in my profession it's important to regulate culinary

ὀψοποιικὴν τέχνην ἐπιθυμίαις καλῶς
χρῆσθαι, ὥστ᾽ ἄνευ νόσου τὴν ἡδονὴν
καρπώσασθαι.

G. καὶ ἐν μουσικῇ δὴ καὶ ἐν ἰατρικῇ καὶ ἐν
τοῖς ἄλλοις πᾶσι καὶ τοῖς ἀνθρωπείοις καὶ
τοῖς θείοις, καθ᾽ ὅσον παρείκει, φυλακτέον
ἑκάτερον τὸν Ἔρωτα· ἔνεστον γάρ. ἐπεὶ καὶ
ἡ τῶν ὡρῶν τοῦ ἐνιαυτοῦ σύστασις μεστή
ἐστιν ἀμφοτέρων τούτων, καὶ ἐπειδὰν μὲν
πρὸς ἄλληλα τοῦ κοσμίου τύχῃ ἔρωτος ἃ
νυνδὴ ἐγὼ ἔλεγον, τά τε θερμὰ καὶ τὰ ψυχρὰ
καὶ ξηρὰ καὶ ὑγρά, καὶ ἁρμονίαν καὶ κρᾶσιν
λάβῃ σώφρονα, ἥκει φέροντα εὐετηρίαν τε
καὶ ὑγίειαν ἀνθρώποις καὶ τοῖς ἄλλοις ζῴοις
τε καὶ φυτοῖς, καὶ οὐδὲν ἠδίκησεν· ὅταν δὲ ὁ
μετὰ τῆς ὕβρεως Ἔρως ἐγκρατέστερος περὶ
τὰς τοῦ ἐνιαυτοῦ ὥρας γένηται, διέφθειρέν
τε πολλὰ καὶ ἠδίκησεν. οἵ τε γὰρ λοιμοὶ
φιλοῦσι γίγνεσθαι ἐκ τῶν τοιούτων καὶ ἄλλα

passions, so that the pleasures of food might be enjoyed without negative consequences for health.

G. In music and medicine, then, and in all the other pursuits that that are adopted on earth and in heaven, we should watch out where appropriate for each kind of Love, as both are potentially present. You can see that even the seasons of the year contain both principles. When the elements I spoke of—hot, cold, dry, and wet—are reconciled by orderly love and are blended in harmony, they bring health and plenty to humans, animals, and plants without harmful effects. But when a more violent kind of Love arises as the seasons turn, it brings great destruction and damage. Plagues and other kinds of disease attack both animals and plants; frost, hail, and blight accompany

ἀνόμοια πολλὰ νοσήματα καὶ τοῖς θηρίοις
καὶ τοῖς φυτοῖς· καὶ γὰρ πάχναι καὶ χάλαζαι
καὶ ἐρυσῖβαι ἐκ πλεονεξίας καὶ ἀκοσμίας
περὶ ἄλληλα τῶν τοιούτων γίγνεται ἐρωτικῶν, ὧν ἐπιστήμη περὶ ἄστρων τε φορὰς καὶ
ἐνιαυτῶν ὥρας ἀστρονομία καλεῖται.

H. ἔτι τοίνυν καὶ αἱ θυσίαι πᾶσαι καὶ οἷς
μαντικὴ ἐπιστατεῖ—ταῦτα δ᾽ ἐστὶν ἡ περὶ
θεούς τε καὶ ἀνθρώπους πρὸς ἀλλήλους
κοινωνία—οὐ περὶ ἄλλο τί ἐστιν ἢ περὶ
Ἔρωτος φυλακήν τε καὶ ἴασιν. πᾶσα γὰρ
ἀσέβεια φιλεῖ γίγνεσθαι ἐὰν μή τις τῷ
κοσμίῳ Ἔρωτι χαρίζηται μηδὲ τιμᾷ τε
αὐτὸν καὶ πρεσβεύῃ ἐν παντὶ ἔργῳ, ἀλλὰ
τὸν ἕτερον, καὶ περὶ γονέας καὶ ζῶντας καὶ
τετελευτηκότας καὶ περὶ θεούς· ἃ δὴ προ-
στέτακται τῇ μαντικῇ ἐπισκοπεῖν τοὺς
ἐρῶντας καὶ ἰατρεύειν, καὶ ἔστιν αὖ ἡ

the excess and disorderliness of the elements. Knowledge of these things in relation to stars and the seasons of the year is the domain of astronomy.

H. In addition, sacrificial ceremonies and everything else in the domain of divination, which is the art of communion between gods and men, involve the preservation of healthy Love and the healing of harmful Love. All impiety is the result of not acquiescing to orderly Eros and failing to honor and give him precedence in every action, but favoring the other kind instead, whether in one's attitude to parents, to the living and the dead, or to the gods. The function of divination is to oversee these kinds of love and to minister to them,

μαντικὴ φιλίας θεῶν καὶ ἀνθρώπων δημι-
ουργὸς τῷ ἐπίστασθαι τὰ κατὰ ἀνθρώπους ἐρωτικά, ὅσα τείνει πρὸς θέμιν καὶ
εὐσέβειαν.

I. οὕτω πολλὴν καὶ μεγάλην, μᾶλλον δὲ
πᾶσαν δύναμιν ἔχει συλλήβδην μὲν ὁ πᾶς
Ἔρως, ὁ δὲ περὶ τἀγαθὰ μετὰ σωφροσύνης
καὶ δικαιοσύνης ἀποτελούμενος καὶ παρ᾽
ἡμῖν καὶ παρὰ θεοῖς, οὗτος τὴν μεγίστην
δύναμιν ἔχει καὶ πᾶσαν ἡμῖν εὐδαιμονίαν
παρασκευάζει καὶ ἀλλήλοις δυναμένους
ὁμιλεῖν καὶ φίλους εἶναι καὶ τοῖς κρείττοσιν
ἡμῶν θεοῖς. [-]

and to foster friendship between gods and men through understanding the operations of love in human life that bring about lawful and reverent behavior.

I. So Love has enormous power, indeed universal power. But the Love that is concerned with goodness and applied with discipline and justice among men and gods is the most powerful of all. It's the source of all happiness for mankind, since it enables us to get along with each other and to be friends, and also to befriend those who are greater than us, the gods. [. . .]

Chapter 4

FINDING ONE'S OTHER HALF: *ARISTOPHANES*

Cured of his hiccups, Aristophanes returns to make a brilliantly comic contribution to the discussion, a fantasy about the meaning of love. Once upon a time, he says, humans were compound creatures, each consisting of either two male or two female halves, or a combination of male and female (*androgyne*, man-woman). These original humans were so strong and self-satisfied that Zeus decided to weaken them by cutting them in two, creating the human species as we are today. Once split, each half was desperate to be reunited with its separate other half, so the new human beings were pacified by being allowed to have intercourse with each other, both for the sake of pleasure and also to perpetuate their race. We human beings, says Aristophanes, still long for our original wholeness; and love is the force that impels each of us to search for our "other half."

Aristophanes' picture is both amusing and appealing, and perhaps it is one that, of all the notions of love presented in the *Symposium*, is most easily recognized by the modern reader. The notion of finding a perfect fit, one's ideal other half, is the stuff of many a romantic tale, play, or film. It is easy to understand how like is drawn to like in love and friendship (even the different sexes of the Aristophanic *androgyne* would be very much alike). When the Roman poet Horace coins a metaphor to reflect his deep feelings for his dear friend Virgil, he calls him "half of my soul" (*animae dimidium meae*).

Aristophanes' speech is also a chance to show that Love doesn't have to be entirely serious and solemn. Just as his fit of hiccups draws attention to bodily functions, Aristophanes suggests that there is something comical about sex and the physical means of indulging in it. Yet that physical act is what allows not only for pleasure but for the perpetuation of the race. Perpetuation of the self in some form, through the creative union brought about by love, offers an answer to the tragic scenario sketched by Phaedrus. For him, the heroic stance of lovers, while presenting an inspired and admirable quality, could be proven only by their death; Aristophanes' comic fantasy restates love's vitality in the pursuit of and creative intimacy with one's "missing half."

Just as Eryximachus has done, Aristophanes suggests that love is a uniting force, but in his case it is one that aims to unite similar, or even virtually identical, elements rather than to harmonize dissimilar ones. It might seem that such a view is retrograde, since Pausanias has already indicated that love can work a creative and ennobling effect only in individuals who differ—whether through the union of young and old, male and female, or educated and unformed. In this case, however, the difference points even more clearly to the notion that love presupposes an inadequacy, a gap that needs to be filled. A human being is really only half a creature, and the longing for the missing half is the desire for completion. It is that urgent desire, Aristophanes proposes, that Eros engenders.

Despite its overt humorousness, then Aristophanes' picture introduces two important new features to the discussion: first, that love emerges out of a lack; and secondly, that it aims at the perpetuation of the individual's qualities through intercourse. Both notions will be picked up and reconfigured in the doctrine attributed to Diotima by Socrates.

Α. ἡ γὰρ πάλαι ἡμῶν φύσις οὐχ αὐτὴ ἦν ἥπερ νῦν, ἀλλ᾽ ἀλλοία. πρῶτον μὲν γὰρ τρία ἦν τὰ γένη τὰ τῶν ἀνθρώπων, οὐχ ὥσπερ νῦν δύο, ἄρρεν καὶ θῆλυ, ἀλλὰ καὶ τρίτον προσῆν κοινὸν ὂν ἀμφοτέρων τούτων, οὗ νῦν ὄνομα λοιπόν, αὐτὸ δὲ ἠφάνισται· ἀνδρόγυνον γὰρ ἓν τότε μὲν ἦν καὶ εἶδος καὶ ὄνομα ἐξ ἀμφοτέ-ρων κοινὸν τοῦ τε ἄρρενος καὶ θήλεος, νῦν δὲ οὐκ ἔστιν ἀλλ᾽ ἢ ἐν ὀνείδει ὄνομα κείμενον. ἔπειτα ὅλον ἦν ἑκάστου τοῦ ἀνθρώπου τὸ εἶδος στρογγύλον, νῶτον καὶ πλευρὰς κύκλῳ ἔχον, χεῖρας δὲ τέτταρας εἶχε, καὶ σκέλη τὰ ἴσα ταῖς χερσίν, καὶ πρόσωπα δύ᾽ ἐπ᾽ αὐ-χένι κυκλοτερεῖ, ὅμοια πάντῃ· κεφαλὴν δ᾽ ἐπ᾽ ἀμφοτέροις τοῖς προσώποις ἐναντίοις κειμένοις μίαν, καὶ ὦτα τέτταρα, καὶ αἰδοῖα δύο, καὶ τἆλλα πάντα ὡς ἀπὸ τούτων ἄν τις

Aristophanes: Translation and Text

A. The original nature of human beings was not what it is today. First, there were three sexes of human, not just the two we have now, male and female, but a third type that combined both of these. A word still exists for it, "androgynous," indicating both male and female, and now used solely as a term of reproach; but at that time there was a type of human that was androgynous in form, which has now vanished. Secondly, the shape of the human being was completely rotund. Its back and its sides were formed in a circle, and it had four hands, four legs, two identical faces on a cylindrical neck, one head with two faces looking in opposite directions, four ears, two sets of genitals, and so on and so forth as you can imagine. It

εἰκάσειεν. ἐπορεύετο δὲ καὶ ὀρθὸν ὥσπερ
νῦν, ὁποτέρωσε βουληθείη· καὶ ὁπότε
ταχὺ ὁρμήσειεν θεῖν, ὥσπερ οἱ κυβιστῶντες
καὶ εἰς ὀρθὸν τὰ σκέλη περιφερόμενοι
κυβιστῶσι κύκλῳ, ὀκτὼ τότε οὖσι τοῖς
μέλεσιν ἀπερειδόμενοι ταχὺ ἐφέροντο
κύκλῳ.

Β. ἦν δὲ διὰ ταῦτα τρία τὰ γένη καὶ
τοιαῦτα, ὅτι τὸ μὲν ἄρρεν ἦν τοῦ ἡλίου τὴν
ἀρχὴν ἔκγονον, τὸ δὲ θῆλυ τῆς γῆς, τὸ δὲ
ἀμφοτέρων μετέχον τῆς σελήνης, ὅτι καὶ ἡ
σελήνη ἀμφοτέρων μετέχει· περιφερῆ δὲ
δὴ ἦν καὶ αὐτὰ καὶ ἡ πορεία αὐτῶν διὰ τὸ
τοῖς γονεῦσιν ὅμοια εἶναι. ἦν οὖν τὴν ἰσχὺν
δεινὰ καὶ τὴν ῥώμην, καὶ τὰ φρονήματα
μεγάλα εἶχον, ἐπεχείρησαν δὲ τοῖς θεοῖς,
καὶ ὃ λέγει Ὅμηρος περὶ Ἐφιάλτου τε καὶ
Ὤτου, περὶ ἐκείνων λέγεται, τὸ εἰς τὸν
οὐρανὸν ἀνάβασιν ἐπιχειρεῖν ποιεῖν, ὡς
ἐπιθησομένων τοῖς θεοῖς.

could walk upright just like now, in what-ever direction it wanted; and when it broke into a run it would revolve rapidly round and round using what were then its eight limbs, the way acrobats fling their legs up and round when they do cartwheels.

   B. The reason there were three sexes was that the male was originally the offspring of the Sun, the female of the Earth, and the man-woman of the Moon (because the moon is part sun and part earth). Both they and the path they travelled were circular, due to their affinity with their parents. They had impressive strength and power, and had big plans, including challenging the gods— Homer tells how Ephialtes and Otus even tried to make a path up to heaven to attack the gods.

ὁ οὖν Ζεὺς καὶ οἱ ἄλλοι θεοὶ ἐβουλεύοντο
ὅτι χρὴ αὐτοὺς ποιῆσαι, καὶ ἠπόρουν· οὔτε
γὰρ ὅπως ἀποκτείναιεν εἶχον καὶ ὥσπερ
τοὺς γίγαντας κεραυνώσαντες τὸ γένος
ἀφανίσαιεν—αἱ τιμαὶ γὰρ αὐτοῖς καὶ ἱερὰ
τὰ παρὰ τῶν ἀνθρώπων ἠφανίζετο—οὔτε
ὅπως ἐῷεν ἀσελγαίνειν.

μόγις δὴ ὁ Ζεὺς ἐννοήσας λέγει ὅτι δοκῶ
μοι, ἔφη, ἔχειν μηχανήν, ὡς ἂν εἶέν τε ἄνθρωποι καὶ παύσαιντο τῆς ἀκολασίας ἀσθενέστε-
ροι γενόμενοι. νῦν μὲν γὰρ αὐτούς, ἔφη,
διατεμῶ δίχα ἕκαστον, καὶ ἅμα μὲν ἀσθενέ-
στεροι ἔσονται, ἅμα δὲ χρησιμώτεροι ἡμῖν
διὰ τὸ πλείους τὸν ἀριθμὸν γεγονέναι· καὶ
βαδιοῦνται ὀρθοὶ ἐπὶ δυοῖν σκελοῖν. ἐὰν δ᾽
ἔτι δοκῶσιν ἀσελγαίνειν καὶ μὴ ᾽θέλωσιν
ἡσυχίαν ἄγειν, πάλιν αὖ, ἔφη, τεμῶ δίχα,
ὥστ᾽ ἐφ᾽ ἑνὸς πορεύσονται σκέλους
ἀσκωλιάζοντες.

Zeus and the other gods debated what they should do with the humans. They were in a quandary because they didn't want to kill them and destroy the race with thunderbolts, as they'd done with the giants, since that would mean an end to the honors and sacrifices they received from humans. But neither could they allow them to defy them unconstrained.

Zeus thought hard and said: I've come up with an idea for weakening human beings so that they can exist without causing us problems. I'll cut them in half. That way they'll not only be weaker, but more useful to us because there'll be more of them. They will walk upright on two legs, but if they continue to make trouble and won't hold their peace, I'll cut them in half again so that they go around hopping on one leg.

C. ταῦτα εἰπὼν ἔτεμνε τοὺς ἀνθρώπους δίχα, ὥσπερ οἱ τὰ ὄα τέμνοντες καὶ μέλλοντες ταριχεύειν, ἢ ὥσπερ οἱ τὰ ᾠὰ ταῖς θριξίν· ὅντινα δὲ τέμοι, τὸν Ἀπόλλω ἐκέλευεν τό τε πρόσωπον μεταστρέφειν καὶ τὸ τοῦ αὐχένος ἥμισυ πρὸς τὴν τομήν, ἵνα θεώμενος τὴν αὑτοῦ τμῆσιν κοσμιώτερος εἴη ὁ ἄνθρωπος, καὶ τἆλλα ἰᾶσθαι ἐκέλευεν. ὁ δὲ τό τε πρόσωπον μετέστρεφε, καὶ συνέλκων πανταχόθεν τὸ δέρμα ἐπὶ τὴν γαστέρα νῦν καλουμένην, ὥσπερ τὰ σύσπαστα βαλλάντια, ἓν στόμα ποιῶν ἀπέδει κατὰ μέσην τὴν γαστέρα, ὃ δὴ τὸν ὀμφαλὸν καλοῦσι. καὶ τὰς μὲν ἄλλας ῥυτίδας τὰς πολλὰς ἐξελέαινε καὶ τὰ στήθη διήρθρου, ἔχων τι τοιοῦτον ὄργανον οἷον οἱ σκυτοτόμοι περὶ τὸν καλάποδα λεαίνοντες τὰς τῶν σκυτῶν ῥυτίδας· ὀλίγας δὲ κατέλιπε, τὰς περὶ αὐτὴν τὴν γαστέρα καὶ τὸν ὀμφαλόν, μνημεῖον εἶναι τοῦ παλαιοῦ πάθους.

C. So saying, he proceeded to cut the human beings in half, as if he were chopping sorb apples in preparation for pickling, or slicing an egg with a hair. He instructed Apollo to turn the face and half of the neck of each sliced human round toward the cut side, so that people would see the cut and act with more humility, and he told him to heal the wounds. Apollo turned the face around and pulled the skin together from all sides, the way you pull a purse shut with drawstrings, to form what we now call the stomach. He made an opening in the center and fastened it with a knot to form what's now the navel. He then smoothed out all the wrinkles and shaped the chest with the tool shoemakers use to smooth out creases in hides on a last, leaving a few wrinkles behind in the area around the stomach and navel so as to remind humans of their primeval state.

D. ἐπειδὴ οὖν ἡ φύσις δίχα ἐτμήθη,
ποθοῦν ἕκαστον τὸ ἥμισυ τὸ αὑτοῦ συνῄει,
καὶ περιβάλλοντες τὰς χεῖρας καὶ συμπλεκό-
μενοι ἀλλήλοις, ἐπιθυμοῦντες συμφῦναι,
ἀπέθνησκον ὑπὸ λιμοῦ καὶ τῆς ἄλλης ἀργίας
διὰ τὸ μηδὲν ἐθέλειν χωρὶς ἀλλήλων ποιεῖν.
καὶ ὁπότε τι ἀποθάνοι τῶν ἡμίσεων, τὸ δὲ
λειφθείη, τὸ λειφθὲν ἄλλο ἐζήτει καὶ συνε-
πλέκετο, εἴτε γυναικὸς τῆς ὅλης ἐντύχοι
ἡμίσει—ὃ δὴ νῦν γυναῖκα καλοῦμεν—εἴτε
ἀνδρός· καὶ οὕτως ἀπώλλυντο.

ἐλεήσας δὲ ὁ Ζεὺς ἄλλην μηχανὴν πορίζε-
ται, καὶ μετατίθησιν αὐτῶν τὰ αἰδοῖα εἰς τὸ
πρόσθεν—τέως γὰρ καὶ ταῦτα ἐκτὸς εἶχον,
καὶ ἐγέννων καὶ ἔτικτον οὐκ εἰς ἀλλήλους
ἀλλ᾽ εἰς γῆν, ὥσπερ οἱ τέττιγες—μετέθηκέ
τε οὖν οὕτω αὐτῶν εἰς τὸ πρόσθεν καὶ διὰ
τούτων τὴν γένεσιν ἐν ἀλλήλοις ἐποίησεν,
διὰ τοῦ ἄρρενος ἐν τῷ θήλει, τῶνδε ἕνεκα,

D. When the original form had been cut in half, each half desperately clung to its other half, and they threw their arms around one another in their desperation to graft themselves back on to each other. They started to die of hunger and general inactivity, because they didn't want to do anything without their other half. When one of the halves died, the one left behind sought out a different half—either half of what was originally female (that is, a woman) or originally male—and clung on to it. And so, they began to die off.

Zeus took pity on them and came up with another plan—to move their genitals to the front. Until then the genitals had been on the far side, and humans had conceived and given birth not by intercourse but by laying offspring into the ground like cicadas. Zeus moved the genitals to the front and

ἵνα ἐν τῇ συμπλοκῇ ἅμα μὲν εἰ ἀνὴρ γυναικὶ
ἐντύχοι, γεννῷεν καὶ γίγνοιτο τὸ γένος, ἅμα
δ᾽ εἰ καὶ ἄρρην ἄρρενι, πλησμονὴ γοῦν
γίγνοιτο τῆς συνουσίας καὶ διαπαύοιντο καὶ
ἐπὶ τὰ ἔργα τρέποιντο καὶ τοῦ ἄλλου βίου
ἐπιμελοῖντο.

E. ἔστι δὴ οὖν ἐκ τόσου ὁ ἔρως ἔμφυτος
ἀλλήλων τοῖς ἀνθρώποις καὶ τῆς ἀρχαίας
φύσεως συναγωγεὺς καὶ ἐπιχειρῶν ποιῆσαι
ἓν ἐκ δυοῖν καὶ ἰάσασθαι τὴν φύσιν τὴν
ἀνθρωπίνην. ἕκαστος οὖν ἡμῶν ἐστιν
ἀνθρώπου σύμβολον, ἅτε τετμημένος
ὥσπερ αἱ ψῆτται, ἐξ ἑνὸς δύο· ζητεῖ δὴ ἀεὶ
τὸ αὑτοῦ ἕκαστος σύμβολον. [-]
    τοῦτο γάρ ἐστι τὸ αἴτιον, ὅτι ἡ ἀρχαία
φύσις ἡμῶν ἦν αὕτη καὶ ἦμεν ὅλοι· τοῦ ὅλου
οὖν τῇ ἐπιθυμίᾳ καὶ διώξει ἔρως ὄνομα.

made humans sow seed through them into each other from male to female, so that if a man had intercourse with a woman they would perpetuate the race, and if it was male on male they would at least have some fun before turning to work and attending to other aspects of life.

E. From ancient times, then, Love for each other has been implanted in human beings, a love that draws us back to our original nature and seeks to make one out of two and so repair human nature. Each of us is a half-token of a human, split like flatfish to make two out of one, and each is constantly looking for his matching token. [. . .]

This is the root cause of our desire to unite: our original nature was like this, and

καὶ πρὸ τοῦ, ὥσπερ λέγω, ἓν ἦμεν, νυνὶ δὲ
διὰ τὴν ἀδικίαν διῳκίσθημεν ὑπὸ τοῦ θεοῦ,
καθάπερ Ἀρκάδες ὑπὸ Λακεδαιμονίων·
φόβος οὖν ἔστιν, ἐὰν μὴ κόσμιοι ὦμεν πρὸς
τοὺς θεούς, ὅπως μὴ καὶ αὖθις διασχισθησό-
μεθα, καὶ περίιμεν ἔχοντες ὥσπερ οἱ ἐν ταῖς
στήλαις καταγραφὴν ἐκτετυπωμένοι,
διαπεπρισμένοι κατὰ τὰς ῥῖνας, γεγονότες
ὥσπερ λίσπαι. ἀλλὰ τούτων ἕνεκα πάντ᾽
ἄνδρα χρὴ ἅπαντα παρακελεύεσθαι εὐσε-
βεῖν περὶ θεούς, ἵνα τὰ μὲν ἐκφύγωμεν, τῶν
δὲ τύχωμεν, ὡς ὁ Ἔρως ἡμῖν ἡγεμὼν καὶ
στρατηγός. [-]

we were wholes; and the name for the desire and pursuit of wholeness is Love.

Before this, as I say, we were one, but now because of our transgressions we've been dispersed by Zeus, the way the Arcadians were dispersed by the Spartans. There's a risk that, if we don't give due deference to the gods, we'll be chopped in two again and go around sawn in half through the nose, like figures carved in relief on gravestones, and will end up like dice cut in half. That's why we should urge reverence of the gods, so that everyone might avoid that fate and enjoy a better one, seeing as Love is our appointed leader and commander. [. . .]

Chapter 5

A STIMULUS TO CREATION: *AGATHON*

The tragic poet Agathon, in whose house the party is taking place, starts by imagining the physical features of the god Eros. Phaedrus had claimed that Eros was the oldest of the gods, but Agathon argues that his softness, beauty, and dexterity prove him to be the youngest. The ambiguity of the terms "old" and "young" is ignored (Phaedrus had argued that Eros was the "oldest" in the sense of being the earliest of the gods to have been born), as the praise of the beautiful young god becomes an overtly rhetorical exercise for the poet.

Agathon rhapsodizes about how everyone becomes a poet at the touch of love.

Eros himself must be a creator and an artist, he says, because love guides and inspires all the arts. Love is beautiful, because beauty is a quality we find in all that is lovely and appealing. Agathon ends with a series of poetic statements about Love couched in the florid rhetorical style associated with the orator Gorgias.

Agathon's speech draws rapturous applause from the audience, but from the reader's point of view it can seem flowery in style and insubstantial in content. It is, however, skillfully composed by Plato to reflect many aspects of what has previously been said and to foreshadow some of what is to come. Just as Pausanias, for instance, has argued that "good" love allows the beloved to provide favors to his lover, Agathon appeals to the view that all's fair in love as long as the conditions are mutually agreed. In attributing courage and moderation to love, his speech looks back both to the speeches of the martial-minded Phaedrus and the puritanical Pausanias, and also hints at the qualities that we will eventually learn characterize Socrates himself.

What is new is the emphasis on beauty and love's power to bring renown and success. None of the speakers so far have made explicit the essential connection of beauty with love. How important is it? On one level, it is uncontroversial that the quality that attracts people to those they love might be called beauty, since in any case, as the saying goes, beauty is in the eye of the beholder. But a marker is laid down here that was earlier touched on by Pausanias and will be picked up by Diotima's speech: love begins with physical attraction.

Secondly, the notion that love generates both offspring and creative achievements will be central to Diotima's doctrine and to her eventual definition of love in terms of both creativity and beauty. We have learned from the start of the *Symposium* that love is an inspiration, but here we are told that the product of that inspiration need not simply be death as understood by Phaedrus, or the desire for harmony and completeness as suggested in different ways by Eryximachus and Aristophanes. Agathon, the successful tragedian, reminds the listeners that there are creative achievements that will outlive their creators, and that artistic products touched with the power of Eros are the ones that will bring lasting renown. In making Agathon speak of the enduring qualities of great art inspired by love, Plato surely has in mind the very dialogue he is in the process of writing.

Α. [-] νεώτατος μὲν δή ἐστι καὶ ἁπαλώτα-
τος, πρὸς δὲ τούτοις ὑγρὸς τὸ εἶδος. οὐ γὰρ
ἂν οἷός τ᾽ ἦν πάντῃ περιπτύσσεσθαι οὐδὲ
διὰ πάσης ψυχῆς καὶ εἰσιὼν τὸ πρῶτον
λανθάνειν καὶ ἐξιών, εἰ σκληρὸς ἦν. συμμέ-
τρου δὲ καὶ ὑγρᾶς ἰδέας μέγα τεκμήριον ἡ
εὐσχημοσύνη, ὃ δὴ διαφερόντως ἐκ πάντων ὁμολογουμένως Ἔρως ἔχει· ἀσχημο-
σύνῃ γὰρ καὶ Ἔρωτι πρὸς ἀλλήλους ἀεὶ
πόλεμος. χρόας δὲ κάλλος ἡ κατ᾽ ἄνθη
δίαιτα τοῦ θεοῦ σημαίνει· ἀνανθεῖ γὰρ καὶ
ἀπηνθηκότι καὶ σώματι καὶ ψυχῇ καὶ ἄλλῳ
ὁτῳοῦν οὐκ ἐνίζει Ἔρως, οὗ δ᾽ ἂν εὐανθής
τε καὶ εὐώδης τόπος ᾖ, ἐνταῦθα δὲ καὶ ἵζει
καὶ μένει.

Β. περὶ μὲν οὖν κάλλους τοῦ θεοῦ καὶ
ταῦτα ἱκανὰ καὶ ἔτι πολλὰ λείπεται, περὶ δὲ

Agathon: Translation and Text

A. [. . .] Eros is truly the youngest and most tender of the gods, and what's more he's a shape-shifter. If he were solid, he wouldn't be able to infiltrate everywhere or steal in and out of people's souls undetected. He must have a well-proportioned and flexible form because he's universally known for his grace; Love and ugliness are at permanent war with one another. The fact that the god lives among flowers speaks to the beauty of his complexion: Eros doesn't settle in a body or soul or anything lacking in bloom or whose flower is fading, but chooses places filled with blossoms and scents and makes his home there.

B. That's enough about Love's beauty, though of course there's more to be said.

ἀρετῆς Ἔρωτος μετὰ ταῦτα λεκτέον, τὸ μὲν
μέγιστον ὅτι Ἔρως οὔτ᾽ ἀδικεῖ οὔτ᾽ ἀδι-
κεῖται οὔτε ὑπὸ θεοῦ οὔτε θεόν, οὔτε ὑπ᾽
ἀνθρώπου οὔτε ἄνθρωπον. οὔτε γὰρ αὐτὸς
βίᾳ πάσχει, εἴ τι πάσχει—βία γὰρ Ἔρωτος
οὐχ ἅπτεται· οὔτε ποιῶν ποιεῖ—πᾶς γὰρ
ἑκὼν Ἔρωτι πᾶν ὑπηρετεῖ, ἃ δ᾽ ἂν ἑκὼν
ἑκόντι ὁμολογήσῃ, φασὶν "οἱ πόλεως
βασιλῆς νόμοι" δίκαια εἶναι.

πρὸς δὲ τῇ δικαιοσύνῃ σωφροσύνης
πλείστης μετέχει. εἶναι γὰρ ὁμολογεῖται
σωφροσύνη τὸ κρατεῖν ἡδονῶν καὶ ἐπιθυμιῶν, Ἔρωτος δὲ μηδεμίαν ἡδονὴν
κρείττω εἶναι· εἰ δὲ ἥττους, κρατοῖντ᾽ ἂν ὑπὸ
Ἔρωτος, ὁ δὲ κρατοῖ, κρατῶν δὲ ἡδονῶν
καὶ ἐπιθυμιῶν ὁ Ἔρως διαφερόντως ἂν
σωφρονοῖ. καὶ μὴν εἴς γε ἀνδρείαν Ἔρωτι
"οὐδ᾽ Ἄρης ἀνθίσταται." οὐ γὰρ ἔχει Ἔρωτα

I'll now speak about the god's excellence. Love's greatest excellence is that he does no harm to god or man, nor can he be harmed by any god or man. Whatever's done to him, it cannot be done by force, because there's no forcing Love. Equally, he doesn't apply force to anyone, because people willingly serve Love in every way, and what one agrees to do willingly is just and right according to the laws that are "the rulers of the city."

In addition to being just, Eros possesses great moderation. Moderation means the control of pleasures and desires, and since no pleasure is greater than love, weaker pleasures and desires are under Love's control—which makes Love supreme in moderation. When it comes to courage, "not even Ares offers resistance" to Love. That's because Ares doesn't possess Love, but Love possesses

Ἄρης, ἀλλ᾽ Ἔρως Ἄρη—Ἀφροδίτης, ὡς
λόγος—κρείττων δὲ ὁ ἔχων τοῦ ἐχομένου·
τοῦ δ᾽ ἀνδρειοτάτου τῶν ἄλλων κρατῶν
πάντων ἂν ἀνδρειότατος εἴη.

C. περὶ μὲν οὖν δικαιοσύνης καὶ σωφροσύνης καὶ ἀνδρείας τοῦ θεοῦ εἴρηται, περὶ δὲ
σοφίας λείπεται· ὅσον οὖν δυνατόν, πειρατέον μὴ ἐλλείπειν. καὶ πρῶτον μέν, ἵν᾽ αὖ καὶ
ἐγὼ τὴν ἡμετέραν τέχνην τιμήσω ὥσπερ
Ἐρυξίμαχος τὴν αὑτοῦ, ποιητὴς ὁ θεὸς σοφὸς
οὕτως ὥστε καὶ ἄλλον ποιῆσαι· πᾶς γοῦν
ποιητὴς γίγνεται, "κἂν ἄμουσος ᾖ τὸ πρίν," οὗ
ἂν Ἔρως ἅψηται. ᾧ δὴ πρέπει ἡμᾶς μαρτυ-
ρίῳ χρῆσθαι, ὅτι ποιητὴς ὁ Ἔρως ἀγαθὸς ἐν
κεφαλαίῳ πᾶσαν ποίησιν τὴν κατὰ μουσικήν·
ἃ γάρ τις ἢ μὴ ἔχει ἢ μὴ οἶδεν, οὔτ᾽ ἂν ἑτέρῳ
δοίη οὔτ᾽ ἂν ἄλλον διδάξειεν. καὶ μὲν δὴ τήν
γε τῶν ζῴων ποίησιν πάντων τίς ἐναντιώσε-
ται μὴ οὐχὶ Ἔρωτος εἶναι σοφίαν, ᾗ γίγνεταί

Ares—the myth relates how he's in thrall to Aphrodite. The possessor is always stronger than the possessed; so if Love controls the god who's otherwise reckoned the most resolute, Love must be the most resolute of all.

C. I've spoken about the justice, moderation, and resoluteness of Love, so now it remains to speak of his skill as best I can. First, I should pay tribute to my craft, just as Eryximachus did to his. Love is a poet of such skill that he makes poets of others: everyone Love touches, "even if hitherto uninspired by the Muse," becomes a poet. This shows that in all types of art Love himself is an expert practitioner: you can't pass on something you don't have, or teach something you don't know. Isn't he responsible for the creation of all animals? Doesn't the skill that Love possesses bring all things to life and make them grow?

τε καὶ φύεται πάντα τὰ ζῷα; ἀλλὰ τὴν τῶν
τεχνῶν δημιουργίαν οὐκ ἴσμεν, ὅτι οὗ μὲν ἂν
ὁ θεὸς οὗτος διδάσκαλος γένηται, ἐλλόγιμος
καὶ φανὸς ἀπέβη, οὗ δ᾽ ἂν Ἔρως μὴ ἐφάψη-
ται, σκοτεινός; [-]

    D. ἐπέρχεται δέ μοί τι καὶ ἔμμετρον εἰπεῖν,
ὅτι οὗτός ἐστιν ὁ ποιῶν

    εἰρήνην μὲν ἐν ἀνθρώποις, πελάγει δὲ
        γαλήνην
    νηνεμίαν, ἀνέμων κοίτην ὕπνον τ᾽ ἐνὶ
        κήδει.

οὗτος δὲ ἡμᾶς ἀλλοτριότητος μὲν κενοῖ,
οἰκειότητος δὲ πληροῖ, τὰς τοιάσδε συνόδους
μετ᾽ ἀλλήλων πάσας τιθεὶς συνιέναι, ἐν
ἑορταῖς, ἐν χοροῖς, ἐν θυσίαισι γιγνόμενος
ἡγεμών· πρᾳότητα μὲν πορίζων, ἀγριότητα δ᾽
ἐξορίζων· φιλόδωρος εὐμενείας, ἄδωρος
δυσμενείας· ἵλεως ἀγαθός· θεατὸς σοφοῖς,
ἀγαστὸς θεοῖς· ζηλωτὸς ἀμοίροις, κτητὸς

And don't we observe that the artists instructed by Love are the ones who end up enjoying fame and distinction, while those untouched by Love languish in obscurity? [. . .]

D. Now, the spirit moves me to say something in verse:

Love brings men peace, and lulls the seas
  with tranquil calm,
allaying winds and easing fears with
  slumber's balm.

This is the Love, you see, that relieves us of disaffection and fills us with affection, brings us together at gatherings like this, and acts as our leader in festivals, dances, and sacrifices. Eros holds out gentleness and banishes roughness, is generous with good-will and conveys no ill-will. He's gracious and kind, admired by the wise, esteemed by

εὐμοίροις· τρυφῆς, ἀβρότητος, χλιδῆς,
χαρίτων, ἱμέρου, πόθου πατήρ· ἐπιμελὴς
ἀγαθῶν, ἀμελὴς κακῶν· ἐν πόνῳ, ἐν φόβῳ,
ἐν πόθῳ, ἐν λόγῳ κυβερνήτης, ἐπιβάτης,
παραστάτης τε καὶ σωτὴρ ἄριστος, συμπά-
ντων τε θεῶν καὶ ἀνθρώπων κόσμος,
ἡγεμὼν κάλλιστος καὶ ἄριστος, ᾧ χρὴ
ἕπεσθαι πάντα ἄνδρα ἐφυμνοῦντα καλῶς,
ᾠδῆς μετέχοντα ἣν ᾄδει θέλγων πάντων
θεῶν τε καὶ ἀνθρώπων νόημα. [-]

the gods, envied by those who lack him, precious to those who possess him; he's the father of delicacy and luxury, elegance and charm, longing and desire; he is diligent to do good, vigilant to do no bad; in work and worry, in desire and discourse, he's our foremost guide and defender, ally and savior; he's the glory of gods and men, the best and brightest leader, in whose footsteps every man should follow, loudly singing his praises and joining in the songs with which he charms the minds of gods and men! [. . .]

Chapter 6

THE LADDER TO TRANSCENDENCE: *SOCRATES*

Agathon's speech is received with rousing applause, despite being (at least to our ears) the most artificial and purely rhetorical of all the contributions. Yet, as we have seen, it contains elements that speak to the notions of Eros voiced by previous participants. What if everything the speakers have so far said about love, each with the avowed aim of praising Eros rather than making any more serious claim to being true, contains some partial and provisional truths? If so, there may be a larger, more comprehensive understanding of the topic that needs to be elaborated.

Instead of simply praising Eros, Socrates tells the group, what he proposes to elaborate to them is nothing less than "the truth about love." Socrates is famous for saying that all he knows is that he knows nothing. In this case, however, he claims to have special access to knowledge about no less momentous a subject than love. At the same time, he lets his listeners know that he's presenting not his own wisdom, but something that was revealed to him on unspecified earlier occasions by a "clever woman" who is identified by the name of Diotima of Mantinea (for clues to her identity, see the Excursus below).

A few passages of dialogue have already established that the previous speakers are mistaken about some of their key assumptions about Eros. Socrates gets Agathon to admit that Eros cannot be beautiful, for instance, because only the lack of beauty would lead to a desire for beauty. Diotima will continue in this vein, getting Socrates to agree that though Love cannot be wise or beautiful, neither can he be ignorant or ugly. The intermediate qualities that Love possesses indicate that he is neither god nor mortal, but an intermediate, spiritual being (*daimōn*) who acts as a conduit between mortals and gods.

Agathon has spoken of Love's beauty, and that is the starting point for Diotima. In youth, she tells Socrates, we are attracted by the beauty of another person's body. We soon begin to recognize, however, that beauty exists in many different bodies, and thence we eventually come to understand that inner beauty is more important than looks—a distinction reminiscent of Pausanias's earlier strictures. Love makes us want to improve those we love, just as Pausanias had proposed, and to preserve something lasting with them. This means we want to generate things or people that outlast us—children, ideas, or writings—inspired by the person whose beauty we desire to possess. As if ascending the steps of a ladder, we ascend from physical beauty to the beauty of the soul, which is the realm of moral goodness. Finally, Diotima says, we come to grasp the source of the beauty and goodness, which is the idea of Beauty itself.

Thus, Diotima says, the complete lover arrives at the level of viewing absolute, eternal beauty and goodness, which are free from the pollution of mortality and human life. That is the most noble vision of all, and that is where true love leads. Diotima signals that the final revelation is something that is likely to be alien to Socrates' thought.

In fact, it represents Plato's own developed doctrine of the Theory of Forms (here anachronistically introduced as having been taught by Diotima to Socrates), which proposes that true reality is a transcendent realm of unchanging perfection.

The doctrine harks back to Eryximachus's claims about love as a harmonious universal principle, but it is far more abstract. It removes us from any physical and psychological realities of love to a philosophical vision that few will be able to share or even grasp. That may be good reason for Plato to have the party interrupted by the rowdy arrival of Alcibiades, whose speech about Socrates—the last and the longest in the dialogue—will once again change the atmosphere, bringing the proceedings back to an entirely human perspective on what it means to love and be loved.

Excursus:
Diotima and Aspasia of Miletus

Diotima is sometimes said, on account of her visionary wisdom and a punning connection of "Mantinea" with the Greek word *mantis* ("prophetess"), to be a priestess or seer. No such designation is given in the *Symposium*. Rather, she is described with curious specificity as being an astute, eloquent woman of non-Athenian background who, by participating in or arranging public sacrifices, "contrived to postpone the Great Plague of Athens by ten years." As there is no external evidence for Diotima's existence, it is generally assumed that the character portrayed is a fiction, and that these details are imaginative and insignificant embellishments. Their specificity, however, suggests that they are intended to be clues left by

Plato to show that the figure of Diotima is, at least in part, based on a real person.

At the date indicated by Plato, 439 BCE (ten years before the Great Plague), Athens' leading citizen and general Pericles had committed a dangerously sacrilegious act by failing to bury the bodies of enemy commanders killed after his successful conquest of the island of Samos. It was a crime that, in Greek eyes, might well have caused divine retribution in the form of a plague, and it would have required expiation. Aspasia of Miletus, his de facto wife for more than five years and a dominant figure in his life, was the only non-Athenian woman who would have been in a position to encourage or initiate public sacrifices in order to atone for the crime on his and Athens' behalf. Together with the meaning of the name Diotima—"honored by Zeus" (see above,

p. xxvii)—this creates an unmistakable link to Aspasia in the figure of Diotima.

Aspasia was the most notoriously brilliant woman of her era. Of elite birth (likely a member of the Alcmaeonid clan, as Pericles was), she immigrated to Athens from her native Miletus in Asia Minor as a young woman around 460 BCE. Historical sources report that in Athens she conducted a salon frequented by elite Athenians including Socrates, in which she discoursed on love (not unlike Diotima, though evidently adopting the role of a marital coach and adviser). In due course, she captivated Pericles and came to live with him as wife or partner for over a decade until he died from the plague in 429 BCE. Her high education was noteworthy: in Plato's dialogue *Menexenus*, she is portrayed under her own name as instructing Socrates in how to give a funeral speech.

There it is straightforwardly claimed that she composed the famous Funeral Speech (as reported by the historian Thucydides) delivered by Pericles in 430 BCE.

Suspected of wielding undue influence over Pericles in matters of war and peace, Aspasia was alleged by contemporary comic playwrights to have instigated the brutal campaign against Samos (a trade rival of her native Miletus) in 440–39 BCE, and subsequently to have sparked the Peloponnesian War of 431–404 BCE. The poets labeled her a "prostitute" and "brothel-madam," and while these labels are generally rejected by historians, some have succumbed to designating her a *hetaira*, "courtesan." That term is never used of her in the ancient sources, and is at odds with the respect she is accorded by the sober prose authors Plato and Xenophon.

Plato's purpose in leaving clues that point unmistakably to Aspasia suggest that he considered her responsible for some—though clearly not all—of the doctrine of love that Socrates attributes to Diotima. The initial doctrine, that love begins with but soon transcends physical attraction, is broadly comparable to what we are told of Aspasia's ethical approach to marital love in her salons; and her patriotic embrace of the powerful Pericles, a man twice her age with a notoriously misshapen skull, might indicate her practical commitment to that doctrine. A cut-off point between the earlier, arguably Aspasianic, part of the doctrine and the "Greater Mystery" that follows is indicated when Diotima tells Socrates, "Up to this point, even you might be initiated in the matter of love" (209e5).

The further development of Diotima's doctrine up to the highest rungs of the "ladder of love" involves Plato's introduction of his own Theory of Forms. Nothing that Diotima is made to say about this theory would have been known to (or even approved by) the real Socrates, let alone proposed by Aspasia. Plato will reasonably have concluded that, whatever the relationship of the initial doctrine to Aspasia's own thought, the author of a speech that contains that "higher doctrine" could not go under the name Aspasia. Hence, it seems reasonable to conclude, his creation of the figure of Diotima.

Α. θεῶν οὐδεὶς φιλοσοφεῖ οὐδ᾽ ἐπιθυμεῖ σοφὸς γενέσθαι—ἔστι γάρ—οὐδ᾽ εἴ τις ἄλλος σοφός, οὐ φιλοσοφεῖ. οὐδ᾽ αὖ οἱ ἀμαθεῖς φιλοσοφοῦσιν οὐδ᾽ ἐπιθυμοῦσι σοφοὶ γενέσθαι· αὐτὸ γὰρ τοῦτό ἐστι χαλεπὸν ἀμαθία, τὸ μὴ ὄντα καλὸν κἀγαθὸν μηδὲ φρόνιμον δοκεῖν αὑτῷ εἶναι ἱκανόν. οὔκουν ἐπιθυμεῖ ὁ μὴ οἰόμενος ἐνδεὴς εἶναι οὗ ἂν μὴ οἴηται ἐπιδεῖσθαι.

τίνες οὖν᾽, ἔφην ἐγώ, ʽὦ Διοτίμα, οἱ φιλοσοφοῦντες, εἰ μήτε οἱ σοφοὶ μήτε οἱ ἀμαθεῖς;

δῆλον δή, ἔφη, τοῦτό γε ἤδη καὶ παιδί, ὅτι οἱ μεταξὺ τούτων ἀμφοτέρων, ὧν ἂν εἴη καὶ ὁ Ἔρως.

Socrates: Translation and Text

A. No god is a philosopher or a seeker after wisdom, because the gods are already wise. The gods and the wise don't seek after wisdom, but neither do the ignorant pursue wisdom or strive to become wise. The problem with ignorance is that people who aren't good or clever think they're perfectly fine, and someone who thinks he's not lacking in something feels no need to seek what he doesn't think he lacks.

Who, then, pursues wisdom, Diotima— I asked—if it's neither the wise nor the ignorant?

A child could tell you that, she said. It's those who fall between these; and Love is among their ranks.

B. ἔστιν γὰρ δὴ τῶν καλλίστων ἡ σοφία,
Ἔρως δ᾽ ἐστὶν ἔρως περὶ τὸ καλόν, ὥστε
ἀναγκαῖον Ἔρωτα φιλόσοφον εἶναι, φιλόσοφον δὲ ὄντα μεταξὺ εἶναι σοφοῦ καὶ
ἀμαθοῦς. αἰτία δὲ αὐτῷ καὶ τούτων ἡ γένε-
σις· πατρὸς μὲν γὰρ σοφοῦ ἐστι καὶ εὐπόρου,
μητρὸς δὲ οὐ σοφῆς καὶ ἀπόρου. ἡ μὲν οὖν
φύσις τοῦ δαίμονος, ὦ φίλε Σώκρατες,
αὕτη· ὃν δὲ σὺ ᾠήθης Ἔρωτα εἶναι, θαυμαστὸν οὐδὲν ἔπαθες. ᾠήθης δέ, ὡς ἐμοὶ δοκεῖ
τεκμαιρομένη ἐξ ὧν σὺ λέγεις, τὸ ἐρώμενον
Ἔρωτα εἶναι, οὐ τὸ ἐρῶν· διὰ ταῦτά σοι
οἶμαι πάγκαλος ἐφαίνετο ὁ Ἔρως. καὶ γὰρ
ἔστι τὸ ἐραστὸν τὸ τῷ ὄντι καλὸν καὶ ἁβρὸν
καὶ τέλεον καὶ μακαριστόν· τὸ δέ γε ἐρῶν
ἄλλην ἰδέαν τοιαύτην ἔχον, οἵαν ἐγὼ διῆλ-
θον.᾽ [-]

C. ἔστιν ἄρα συλλήβδην, ἔφη, ὁ ἔρως τοῦ
τὸ ἀγαθὸν αὑτῷ εἶναι ἀεί.

ἀληθέστατα, ἔφην ἐγώ, λέγεις.

B. Wisdom's a thing of great beauty, and *erōs* is the love of what's beautiful. So Eros must be a lover of wisdom, and as a lover of wisdom he falls in between the wise and the ignorant. This is explained by his birth: he comes from a father who's wise and re- sourceful, and a mother who lacks wisdom and resource. That, my dear Socrates, is the nature of the divinity. The way you imagined Eros is not surprising, since from what you say you supposed him to be the beloved rather than the lover, so you imagined Love to be wholly beautiful. The beloved is indeed beautiful, delicate, perfect, and most blessed, but the lover is something else, as I've explained. [. . .]

C. In short, she said, love is the desire always to possess the good.

That's right, I said.

ὅτε δὴ τοῦτο ὁ ἔρως ἐστὶν ἀεί, ἦ δ᾽ ἥ, τῶν
τίνα τρόπον διωκόντων αὐτὸ καὶ ἐν τίνι
πράξει ἡ σπουδὴ καὶ ἡ σύντασις ἔρως ἂν
καλοῖτο; τί τοῦτο τυγχάνει ὂν τὸ ἔργον;
ἔχεις εἰπεῖν;

οὐ μεντἂν σέ, ἔφην ἐγώ, ὦ Διοτίμα,
ἐθαύμαζον ἐπὶ σοφίᾳ καὶ ἐφοίτων παρὰ σὲ
αὐτὰ ταῦτα μαθησόμενος.

ἀλλὰ ἐγώ σοι, ἔφη, ἐρῶ. ἔστι γὰρ τοῦτο
τόκος ἐν καλῷ καὶ κατὰ τὸ σῶμα καὶ κατὰ
τὴν ψυχήν.

μαντείας, ἦν δ᾽ ἐγώ, δεῖται ὅτι ποτε
λέγεις, καὶ οὐ μανθάνω.

ἀλλ᾽ ἐγώ, ἦ δ᾽ ἥ, σαφέστερον ἐρῶ.
κυοῦσιν γάρ, ἔφη, ὦ Σώκρατες, πάντες
ἄνθρωποι καὶ κατὰ τὸ σῶμα καὶ κατὰ τὴν
ψυχήν, καὶ ἐπειδὰν ἔν τινι ἡλικίᾳ γένωνται,
τίκτειν ἐπιθυμεῖ ἡμῶν ἡ φύσις. τίκτειν δὲ ἐν

So since that's what Eros is and always has been, she said, in what kind of pursuit and action do we call our passionate intensity "love"? What is it trying to achieve, can you tell me?

If I could tell you, Diotima, I said, I wouldn't be standing here in awe of your wisdom and hoping to learn the answers from you.

Let me tell you, then, she said. Love is birth in the beautiful, as regards both body and soul.

That needs an interpreter! I said, I don't understand it.

All right, she said, I'll make it clearer. Look, Socrates: all human beings brim with potential offspring in body and in soul. When they reach a certain age it's natural to want to birth that offspring, and one cannot do so in conjunction with ugliness, only

μὲν αἰσχρῷ οὐ δύναται, ἐν δὲ τῷ καλῷ. ἡ
γὰρ ἀνδρὸς καὶ γυναικὸς συνουσία τόκος
ἐστίν. ἔστι δὲ τοῦτο θεῖον τὸ πρᾶγμα, καὶ
τοῦτο ἐν θνητῷ ὄντι τῷ ζῴῳ ἀθάνατον
ἔνεστιν, ἡ κύησις καὶ ἡ γέννησις. τὰ δὲ ἐν τῷ
ἀναρμόστῳ ἀδύνατον γενέσθαι. ἀνάρμο-
στον δ᾽ ἐστὶ τὸ αἰσχρὸν παντὶ τῷ θείῳ, τὸ δὲ
καλὸν ἁρμόττον. [-]

D. δεῖ γάρ, ἔφη, τὸν ὀρθῶς ἰόντα ἐπὶ
τοῦτο τὸ πρᾶγμα ἄρχεσθαι μὲν νέον ὄντα
ἰέναι ἐπὶ τὰ καλὰ σώματα, καὶ πρῶτον μέν,
ἐὰν ὀρθῶς ἡγῆται ὁ ἡγούμενος, ἑνὸς αὐτὸν
σώματος ἐρᾶν καὶ ἐνταῦθα γεννᾶν λόγους
καλούς, ἔπειτα δὲ αὐτὸν κατανοῆσαι ὅτι τὸ
κάλλος τὸ ἐπὶ ὁτῳοῦν σώματι τῷ ἐπὶ ἑτέρῳ
σώματι ἀδελφόν ἐστι, καὶ εἰ δεῖ διώκειν τὸ

with beauty. The union between man and woman leads to procreation, which is a divine process, since the process of pregnancy and giving birth is an immortal principle in living things that are otherwise mortal. But it's impossible for this to happen in relation to something unharmonious. Ugliness is quite out of harmony with the divine, while beauty's in harmony with it. [. . .]

D. To set out on this path properly, one should start in youth to take one's path toward beautiful bodies. If you're guided in the right way, you should first fall in love with a single body, and in conjunction with that body create beautiful thoughts. Eventually, you should come to see that the beauty of any one body is akin to that of any other body, and that if you're in pursuit of physical beauty it's stupid not to recognize that the beauty in any one body

ἐπ᾽ εἴδει καλόν, πολλὴ ἄνοια μὴ οὐχ ἕν
τε καὶ ταὐτὸν ἡγεῖσθαι τὸ ἐπὶ πᾶσιν τοῖς
σώμασι κάλλος· τοῦτο δ᾽ ἐννοήσαντα
καταστῆναι πάντων τῶν καλῶν σωμάτων
ἐραστήν, ἑνὸς δὲ τὸ σφόδρα τοῦτο χαλάσαι
καταφρονήσαντα καὶ σμικρὸν ἡγησάμενον.

μετὰ δὲ ταῦτα τὸ ἐν ταῖς ψυχαῖς κάλλος
τιμιώτερον ἡγήσασθαι τοῦ ἐν τῷ σώματι,
ὥστε καὶ ἐὰν ἐπιεικὴς ὢν τὴν ψυχήν τις κἂν
σμικρὸν ἄνθος ἔχῃ, ἐξαρκεῖν αὐτῷ καὶ ἐρᾶν
καὶ κήδεσθαι καὶ τίκτειν λόγους τοιούτους
καὶ ζητεῖν, οἵτινες ποιήσουσι βελτίους τοὺς
νέους, ἵνα ἀναγκασθῇ αὖ θεάσασθαι τὸ ἐν
τοῖς ἐπιτηδεύμασι καὶ τοῖς νόμοις καλὸν καὶ
τοῦτ᾽ ἰδεῖν ὅτι πᾶν αὐτὸ αὑτῷ συγγενές
ἐστιν, ἵνα τὸ περὶ τὸ σῶμα καλὸν σμικρόν τι
ἡγήσηται εἶναι.

Ε. μετὰ δὲ τὰ ἐπιτηδεύματα ἐπὶ τὰς
ἐπιστήμας ἀγαγεῖν, ἵνα ἴδῃ αὖ ἐπιστημῶν

is the same as the beauty in another. Recognizing this will allow you to relax your intense feelings for a single body and to put that in perspective as something inconsequential, and will make you a lover of all beautiful bodies.

In the next stage, you should recognize that beauty of the mind is worth more than bodily beauty, so that if someone has a truly worthy soul, even though he's less attractive physically, that's good reason to love him and have feelings for him, and to search out fine thoughts that will improve young men. They in turn will be compelled to contemplate the beauty of social practices and institutions and see how all of these are interconnected, and will come to view bodily beauty as a trifling thing.

E. After laws and institutions, the guide should direct the lover toward the various

κάλλος, καὶ βλέπων πρὸς πολὺ ἤδη τὸ
καλὸν μηκέτι τὸ παρ᾽ ἑνί, ὥσπερ οἰκέτης,
ἀγαπῶν παιδαρίου κάλλος ἢ ἀνθρώπου
τινὸς ἢ ἐπιτηδεύματος ἑνός, δουλεύων
φαῦλος ᾖ καὶ σμικρολόγος, ἀλλ᾽ ἐπὶ τὸ
πολὺ πέλαγος τετραμμένος τοῦ καλοῦ καὶ
θεωρῶν πολλοὺς καὶ καλοὺς λόγους καὶ
μεγαλοπρεπεῖς τίκτῃ καὶ διανοήματα ἐν
φιλοσοφίᾳ ἀφθόνῳ, ἕως ἂν ἐνταῦθα ῥω-
σθεὶς καὶ αὐξηθεὶς κατίδῃ τινὰ ἐπιστήμην
μίαν τοιαύτην, ἥ ἐστι καλοῦ τοιοῦδε.

πειρῶ δέ μοι, ἔφη, τὸν νοῦν προσέχειν ὡς
οἷόν τε μάλιστα. ὃς γὰρ ἂν μέχρι ἐνταῦθα
πρὸς τὰ ἐρωτικὰ παιδαγωγηθῇ, θεώμενος
ἐφεξῆς τε καὶ ὀρθῶς τὰ καλά, πρὸς τέλος
ἤδη ἰὼν τῶν ἐρωτικῶν ἐξαίφνης κατόψεταί
τι θαυμαστὸν τὴν φύσιν καλόν, τοῦτο ἐκεῖνο,
ὦ Σώκρατες, οὗ δὴ ἕνεκεν καὶ οἱ ἔμπροσθεν
πάντες πόνοι ἦσαν, πρῶτον μὲν ἀεὶ ὂν καὶ
οὔτε γιγνόμενον οὔτε ἀπολλύμενον, οὔτε

sciences so that he recognizes their beauty, and in contemplating the variety of beauty he'll no longer slavishly and narrow-mindedly fixate on the beauty of one boy or person or particular pursuit. Instead, turning toward the open sea of beauty and contemplating it, he'll give birth to fine and noble thoughts in his unstinting pursuit of wisdom until, standing strong and vigorous, he comes to enjoy a vision of a single kind of knowledge of the beauty, which I shall now describe.

Try now, Diotima said, to pay close attention to what I'm saying. Whoever has been instructed in love up to this point by observing beautiful things in due order and in the right way, will now approach the final shore of love, and will suddenly behold a wondrous beauty—the goal, Socrates, of all his previous efforts. This beauty is, first,

αὐξανόμενον οὔτε φθίνον, ἔπειτα οὐ τῇ μὲν
καλόν, τῇ δ᾽ αἰσχρόν, οὐδὲ τοτὲ μέν, τοτὲ δὲ
οὔ, οὐδὲ πρὸς μὲν τὸ καλόν, πρὸς δὲ τὸ
αἰσχρόν, οὐδ᾽ ἔνθα μὲν καλόν, ἔνθα δὲ
αἰσχρόν, ὡς τισὶ μὲν ὂν καλόν, τισὶ δὲ
αἰσχρόν.

F. οὐδ᾽ αὖ φαντασθήσεται αὐτῷ τὸ καλὸν
οἷον πρόσωπόν τι οὐδὲ χεῖρες οὐδὲ ἄλλο
οὐδὲν ὧν σῶμα μετέχει, οὐδέ τις λόγος οὐδέ
τις ἐπιστήμη, οὐδέ που ὂν ἐν ἑτέρῳ τινι, οἷον
ἐν ζώῳ ἢ ἐν γῇ ἢ ἐν οὐρανῷ ἢ ἔν τῳ ἄλλῳ,
ἀλλ᾽ αὐτὸ καθ᾽ αὑτὸ μεθ᾽ αὑτοῦ μονοειδὲς
ἀεὶ ὄν, τὰ δὲ ἄλλα πάντα καλὰ ἐκείνου μετέχοντα τρόπον τινὰ τοιοῦτον, οἷον γιγνομένων
τε τῶν ἄλλων καὶ ἀπολλυμένων μηδὲν ἐκεῖνο
μήτε τι πλέον μήτε ἔλαττον γίγνεσθαι μηδὲ
πάσχειν μηδέν.
ὅταν δή τις ἀπὸ τῶνδε διὰ τὸ ὀρθῶς
παιδεραστεῖν ἐπανιὼν ἐκεῖνο τὸ καλὸν

everlasting, and neither comes into being and passes away or waxes and wanes. Secondly, it's not beautiful in one respect and ugly in another, or beautiful at one time and not at another, or beautiful on one account and not another, or in one context and not another, or to some people and not to others.

F. Beauty won't be seen as a face or hands or any part of a body, or a speech or piece of knowledge, or something that exists in any creature that lives on earth or flies in the sky or anywhere else. Absolute and separate, it's an eternal single form, and all beautiful things share in it in such a way that, while other things come into being and pass away, it does not grow or wane or undergo any changes.

When someone who has risen through these stages by loving boys correctly catches sight of that beauty, he will be close to the

ἄρχηται καθορᾶν, σχεδὸν ἄν τι ἅπτοιτο τοῦ
τέλους. τοῦτο γὰρ δή ἐστι τὸ ὀρθῶς ἐπὶ τὰ
ἐρωτικὰ ἰέναι ἢ ὑπ᾽ ἄλλου ἄγεσθαι, ἀρχόμε-
νον ἀπὸ τῶνδε τῶν καλῶν ἐκείνου ἕνεκα τοῦ
καλοῦ ἀεὶ ἐπανιέναι, ὥσπερ ἐπαναβασμοῖς
χρώμενον, ἀπὸ ἑνὸς ἐπὶ δύο καὶ ἀπὸ δυοῖν
ἐπὶ πάντα τὰ καλὰ σώματα, καὶ ἀπὸ τῶν
καλῶν σωμάτων ἐπὶ τὰ καλὰ ἐπιτηδεύματα,
καὶ ἀπὸ τῶν ἐπιτηδευμάτων ἐπὶ τὰ καλὰ
μαθήματα, καὶ ἀπὸ τῶν μαθημάτων ἐπ᾽
ἐκεῖνο τὸ μάθημα τελευτῆσαι, ὅ ἐστιν οὐκ
ἄλλου ἢ αὐτοῦ ἐκείνου τοῦ καλοῦ μάθημα,
καὶ γνῷ αὐτὸ τελευτῶν ὃ ἔστι καλόν.

G. ἐνταῦθα τοῦ βίου, ὦ φίλε Σώκρατες,
ἔφη ἡ Μαντινικὴ ξένη, εἴπερ που ἄλλοθι,
βιωτὸν ἀνθρώπῳ, θεωμένῳ αὐτὸ τὸ καλόν.
ὃ ἐάν ποτε ἴδης, οὐ κατὰ χρυσίον τε καὶ
ἐσθῆτα καὶ τοὺς καλοὺς παῖδάς τε καὶ
νεανίσκους δόξει σοι εἶναι, οὓς νῦν ὁρῶν

goal. This is the correct way to approach love or be directed to it by someone else. One begins with beautiful things on earth and passes upward for the sake of that higher beauty, using these as steps that lead from one to two and from two to all beautiful bodies, and from beautiful bodies to beautiful pursuits, and from pursuits to beautiful kinds of learning, and from that learning to the knowledge that is none other than that of beauty itself, where one may finally know the essence of beauty.

G. This, my dear Socrates, said the Mantinean woman, is the life that above all a man should live, one spent in contemplation of absolute beauty. If you were to see that, you'd find that gold or clothes cannot compare, or the lovely boys and youngsters

ἐκπέπληξαι καὶ ἕτοιμος εἶ καὶ σὺ καὶ ἄλλοι
πολλοί, ὁρῶντες τὰ παιδικὰ καὶ συνόντες
ἀεὶ αὐτοῖς, εἴ πως οἷόν τ᾽ ἦν, μήτ᾽ ἐσθίειν
μήτε πίνειν, ἀλλὰ θεᾶσθαι μόνον καὶ
συνεῖναι.

τί δῆτα, ἔφη, οἰόμεθα, εἴ τῳ γένοιτο
αὐτὸ τὸ καλὸν ἰδεῖν εἰλικρινές, καθαρόν,
ἄμεικτον, ἀλλὰ μὴ ἀνάπλεων σαρκῶν τε
ἀνθρωπίνων καὶ χρωμάτων καὶ ἄλλης
πολλῆς φλυαρίας θνητῆς, ἀλλ᾽ αὐτὸ τὸ
θεῖον καλὸν δύναιτο μονοειδὲς κατιδεῖν;
ἆρ᾽ οἴει, ἔφη, φαῦλον βίον γίγνεσθαι
ἐκεῖσε βλέποντος ἀνθρώπου καὶ ἐκεῖνο ᾧ
δεῖ θεωμένου καὶ συνόντος αὐτῷ; ἢ οὐκ
ἐνθυμῇ, ἔφη, ὅτι ἐνταῦθα αὐτῷ μοναχοῦ
γενήσεται, ὁρῶντι ᾧ ὁρατὸν τὸ καλόν,
τίκτειν οὐκ εἴδωλα ἀρετῆς, ἅτε οὐκ εἰδώ-
λου ἐφαπτομένῳ, ἀλλὰ ἀληθῆ, ἅτε τοῦ
ἀληθοῦς ἐφαπτομένῳ· τεκόντι δὲ ἀρετὴν

who now leave you spellbound when you look at them, those sweethearts for whose sake you and many others would happily forgo food and drink were it possible, just to gaze on them and spend every minute by their side.

But what might we think if we could see beauty itself, pure, simple, unalloyed, undefiled by human flesh and color and all other mortal vanities? If we could contemplate divine beauty in its simple, unique form? Do you think life would be a worthless thing if a person could look at that, contemplate it as he should, and connect with it? Don't you see that only then, when you grasp that beauty through the medium that makes it visible, would you give birth not to images of excellence but to true excellence, since you'd be in touch not with mere images but

ἀληθῆ καὶ θρεψαμένῳ ὑπάρχει θεοφιλεῖ
γενέσθαι, καὶ εἴπέρ τῳ ἄλλῳ ἀνθρώπων
ἀθανάτῳ καὶ ἐκείνῳ; [-]

with reality? And after giving birth to true excellence and fostering it, don't you think you'd be truly beloved of the gods, and might even aspire to becoming immortal insofar as any mortal can? [. . .]

Chapter 7

LOVE IS WHO YOU LOVE:
ALCIBIADES

Some say a troop of cavalry
or marching men, or ships of war,
the finest sight on this dark earth;
I say it's who you love.

Sappho (fr. 16.1–4)

After Diotima's mystical revelation of the truth about love, Alcibiades crashes in on the party and embarks on a passionate speech in praise of Socrates. His warm, personal testimony to Socrates' character and actions changes the atmosphere from the metaphysical to the personal; he describes his mentor as a man who inspires and offers love of the best kind. Outwardly Socrates is ugly, Alcibiades tells his listeners, with his snub nose and bulging eyes, but within him there is true beauty.

Alcibiades recounts how Socrates refused to take advantage of a sexual relationship with him, handsome as he was, because he cared only for his soul. The philosopher's fortitude showed itself in his conduct on military campaigns, when he would walk barefoot through ice and snow unaffected and did not yield to feelings of hunger or cold. This is a man whom one can love and admire without reserve, says Alcibiades. The kind of love that he gives in return is pure and unconditional.

Many of the themes raised by previous speakers are woven into Alcibiades' description. In battle, Socrates put himself in mortal danger to save the life of his beloved friend, just as Phaedrus would expect a lover to do. In caring for Alcibiades' improvement rather than accepting the sexual favors he offered, Socrates exemplified the Heavenly Aphrodite praised by Pausanias. In balancing the need for food, drink, and exercise, Socrates is presented as a supreme example of health of the kind that the physician Eryximachus would approve. As for the "other half" that Aristophanes comically portrays as fulfilling the nature of the original human, in many ways the younger Alcibiades—ambitious, clever, and proud of his military prowess—presents himself as an alter ego of the philosopher. However, Socrates has moved on in his pursuit of wisdom, while Alcibiades ruefully admits that he has not become the virtuous person Socrates would want him to be.

Socrates also appears to be a source of creativity and goodness, the functions that

Agathon attributed to Eros. When Socrates first arrived at Agathon's house, where the banquet was being held, the playwright jocularly remarked that he hoped that he might acquire some of the philosopher's wisdom by sitting next to him. Socrates rebuffed the idea by saying that wisdom cannot pass from one person to another like water through a woolen thread (by what we call "capillary action"). Alcibiades says, however, that in the presence of Socrates he was always able to keep his mind on higher things, and that only when he strayed from Socrates' good influence did he fall into error.

The historical circumstances hinted at by Alcibiades' admission would have been known to many of Plato's readers. Alcibiades' conduct during the Peloponnesian War (431–404 BCE), when his defection to the Spartan enemy for a time caused incalculable damage to his city's cause, meant that he was remembered as, at best, an ambiguous figure, and, at worst, a hated traitor to Athens. Plato wished to exonerate Socrates of any blame for Alcibiades' conduct by putting into the latter's mouth the disavowal of any Socratic influence on the actions for which he was reviled. Those actions, nonetheless, formed part of the reason that Socrates was tried, convicted, and executed in 399 BCE on charges that included "corrupting young men."

Such young men would have been identified as those inimical to the Athenian democratic constitution, as Alcibiades was widely held to be. Diotima has already been made to suggest that Socrates was no such corrupter (see section D of Socrates' speech above), either sexually or politically, when she instructs him: "You should recognize that beauty of the mind is worth more than bodily beauty, so that if someone has a truly worthy soul, even though he's less attractive physically, that's reason to love him and have feelings for him and to search out fine thoughts that will *improve young men*. They in turn will be compelled to contemplate *the beauty of social practices and institutions* and see how all of these are interconnected, and *will view bodily beauty as a trifling thing*" (emphasis added). Alcibiades' speech is designed to offer further proof of Socrates' blamelessness.

The way the dialogue ends leaves us with a difficult question. Which depiction of love does Plato expect the reader to accept as authoritative, that of Socrates or that of Alcibiades? In Greek literature, the last speaker is commonly considered to be the last word on any topic. Does that mean that Plato is happy for us to put aside the ultimately high-flown metaphysics of Socrates' contribution in favor of the human picture of intimate mutual friendship depicted by Alcibiades?

Perhaps there is room for both. We may continue to ask questions about the meaning of love, but philosophy can take us only so far. Rational analysis is prone to being overtaken by personal feelings and lived experience. Part of that experience, however, should be to think—and talk—about the meaning of love. That is the course that Plato's *Symposium* invites us to pursue.

Α. προκαλοῦμαι δὴ αὐτὸν πρὸς τὸ συνδει-
πνεῖν, ἀτεχνῶς ὥσπερ ἐραστὴς παιδικοῖς
ἐπιβουλεύων. καί μοι οὐδὲ τοῦτο ταχὺ
ὑπήκουσεν, ὅμως δ᾽ οὖν χρόνῳ ἐπείσθη.
ἐπειδὴ δὲ ἀφίκετο τὸ πρῶτον, δειπνήσας
ἀπιέναι ἐβούλετο. καὶ τότε μὲν αἰσχυνόμε-
νος ἀφῆκα αὐτόν· αὖθις δ᾽ ἐπιβουλεύσας,
ἐπειδὴ ἐδεδειπνήκεμεν διελεγόμην ἀεὶ
πόρρω τῶν νυκτῶν, καὶ ἐπειδὴ ἐβούλετο
ἀπιέναι, σκηπτόμενος ὅτι ὀψὲ εἴη, προσηνά-
γκασα αὐτὸν μένειν. ἀνεπαύετο οὖν ἐν τῇ
ἐχομένῃ ἐμοῦ κλίνῃ, ἐν ᾗπερ ἐδείπνει, καὶ
οὐδεὶς ἐν τῷ οἰκήματι ἄλλος καθηῦδεν ἢ
ἡμεῖς.

μέχρι μὲν οὖν δὴ δεῦρο τοῦ λόγου
καλῶς ἂν ἔχοι καὶ πρὸς ὁντινοῦν λέγειν· τὸ

Alcibiades: Translation and Text

A. Just like a lover setting out to ensnare a young flame, I invited Socrates to have dinner with me. He didn't respond straight away, but in the end he accepted. That first time he came to dinner, he got up to leave right after the meal, and I didn't have the nerve to detain him. The next time I was more strategic. After dinner, I kept talking late into the night, and when Socrates was getting ready to leave, I persuaded him that he'd be better off staying since it was late. So he readied himself to sleep on the couch next to mine on which he'd reclined at dinner. No one but ourselves were sleeping in the room.

Look, up to this point it wouldn't matter who heard this story, but if I were sober you

δ᾽ ἐντεῦθεν οὐκ ἄν μου ἠκούσατε λέγοντος,
εἰ μὴ πρῶτον μέν, τὸ λεγόμενον, οἶνος ἄνευ
τε παίδων καὶ μετὰ παίδων ἦν ἀληθής,
ἔπειτα ἀφανίσαι Σωκράτους ἔργον ὑπερή-
φανον εἰς ἔπαινον ἐλθόντα ἄδικόν μοι
φαίνεται. ἔτι δὲ τὸ τοῦ δηχθέντος ὑπὸ τοῦ
ἔχεως πάθος κἄμ᾽ ἔχει. φασὶ γάρ πού τινα
τοῦτο παθόντα οὐκ ἐθέλειν λέγειν οἷον ἦν
πλὴν τοῖς δεδηγμένοις, ὡς μόνοις γνωσομέ-
νοις τε καὶ συγγνωσομένοις εἰ πᾶν ἐτόλμα
δρᾶν τε καὶ λέγειν ὑπὸ τῆς ὀδύνης.

Β. ἐγὼ οὖν δεδηγμένος τε ὑπὸ ἀλγεινοτέ-
ρου καὶ τὸ ἀλγεινότατον ὧν ἄν τις δηχθείη—
τὴν καρδίαν γὰρ ἢ ψυχὴν ἢ ὅτι δεῖ αὐτὸ
ὀνομάσαι πληγείς τε καὶ δηχθεὶς ὑπὸ τῶν ἐν
φιλοσοφίᾳ λόγων, οἳ ἔχονται ἐχίδνης
ἀγριώτερον, νέου ψυχῆς μὴ ἀφυοῦς ὅταν
λάβωνται, καὶ ποιοῦσι δρᾶν τε καὶ λέγειν

wouldn't catch me telling you this next part, even if the slaves weren't here listening. But *in vino veritas*, as they say; and it would be wrong to suppress details of Socrates' high-handed behavior given that I'm about to sing his praises. What's more, you know what they say about people who've been bitten by a snake. They don't want to talk about it to anyone but other people who've experienced snakebite, since they're the only ones who'll understand and excuse them for what they will do and say because of the pain.

B. Well, I've been bitten by something even more painful than snakebite, and in the most tender place. I've been stung in my heart or my soul, whatever you choose to call it, by the arrows of philosophy. Those darts are sharper than a serpent's tooth! They get lodged in the minds of susceptible

ότιοῦν—καὶ ὁρῶν αὖ Φαίδρους, Ἀγάθωνας,
Ἐρυξιμάχους, Παυσανίας, Ἀριστοδήμους τε
καὶ Ἀριστοφάνας· Σωκράτη δὲ αὐτὸν τί δεῖ
λέγειν, καὶ ὅσοι ἄλλοι; πάντες γὰρ κεκοινω-
νήκατε τῆς φιλοσόφου μανίας τε καὶ
βακχείας—διὸ πάντες ἀκούσεσθε· συγγνώ-
σεσθε γὰρ τοῖς τε τότε πραχθεῖσι καὶ τοῖς
νῦν λεγομένοις. οἱ δὲ οἰκέται, καὶ εἴ τις
ἄλλος ἐστὶν βέβηλός τε καὶ ἄγροικος, πύλας
πάνυ μεγάλας τοῖς ὠσὶν ἐπίθεσθε.

C. ἐπειδὴ γὰρ οὖν, ὦ ἄνδρες, ὅ τε λύχνος
ἀπεσβήκει καὶ οἱ παῖδες ἔξω ἦσαν, ἔδοξέ μοι
χρῆναι μηδὲν ποικίλλειν πρὸς αὐτόν, ἀλλ᾽
ἐλευθέρως εἰπεῖν ἅ μοι ἐδόκει· καὶ εἶπον
κινήσας αὐτόν, Σώκρατες, καθεύδεις;
οὐ δῆτα, ἦ δ᾽ ὅς.
οἶσθα οὖν ἅ μοι δέδοκται;

young men, making them do and say any-thing—yes, I'm looking at you, Phaedrus, and you Agathon, and Eryximachus, Pausa-nias, Aristodemus, and Aristophanes! Not to mention Socrates and everyone else who's here. You've all experienced the madness and excitement of philosophy. So hear me out. I know you'll excuse what I did then and what I'm going to say now. But the servants should block their ears, as should anyone who's unsympathetic or unsophisticated.

C. To continue my story:

When the lamp had been put out and the slaves had gone away, I decided to dispense with all ambiguity and make my intentions clear. So I shook him and said, Socrates, are you asleep?

No, he said.

You know what I've decided?

No, what? he said.

τί μάλιστα, ἔφη.

σὺ ἐμοὶ δοκεῖς, ἦν δ᾽ ἐγώ, ἐμοῦ ἐραστὴς ἄξιος γεγονέναι μόνος, καί μοι φαίνῃ ὀκνεῖν μνησθῆναι πρός με. ἐγὼ δὲ οὑτωσὶ ἔχω· πάνυ ἀνόητον ἡγοῦμαι εἶναι σοὶ μὴ οὐ καὶ τοῦτο χαρίζεσθαι καὶ εἴ τι ἄλλο ἢ τῆς οὐσίας τῆς ἐμῆς δέοιο ἢ τῶν φίλων τῶν ἐμῶν. ἐμοὶ μὲν γὰρ οὐδέν ἐστι πρεσβύτερον τοῦ ὡς ὅτι βέλτιστον ἐμὲ γενέσθαι, τούτου δὲ οἶμαί μοι συλλήπτορα οὐδένα κυριώτερον εἶναι σοῦ. ἐγὼ δὴ τοιούτῳ ἀνδρὶ πολὺ μᾶλλον ἂν μὴ χαριζόμενος αἰσχυνοίμην τοὺς φρονίμους, ἢ χαριζόμενος τούς τε πολλοὺς καὶ ἄφρονας.

D. καὶ οὗτος ἀκούσας μάλα εἰρωνικῶς καὶ σφόδρα ἑαυτοῦ τε καὶ εἰωθότως ἔλεξεν ʽὦ φίλε Ἀλκιβιάδη, κινδυνεύεις τῷ ὄντι οὐ φαῦλος εἶναι, εἴπερ ἀληθῆ τυγχάνει ὄντα ἃ λέγεις περὶ ἐμοῦ, καί τις ἔστ᾽ ἐν ἐμοὶ δύνα-μις δι᾽ ἧς ἂν σὺ γένοιο ἀμείνων· ἀμήχανόν

Of all my lovers you're the only one I consider worthy of me. But you're holding back from claiming what's due to you. Here's where I stand: I'd be a fool not to grant you that favor, or whatever else you might want. In fact, I want to give you anything that I or my friends can offer you. Nothing's more important to me than to become the best person I can be, and no one's more capable of helping me do that than you. I'd feel bad if people I respect thought I was denying myself to a man such as you. Much worse than I would feel if the foolish masses out there assumed otherwise!

D. Socrates replied with his characteristic ironic humor:

My dear Alcibiades, it would be very impressive if what you say were true—that I'm somehow able to make you a better man. That would mean that you can see in

τοι κάλλος ὁρῴης ἂν ἐν ἐμοὶ καὶ τῆς παρὰ
σοὶ εὐμορφίας πάμπολυ διαφέρον. εἰ δὴ
καθορῶν αὐτὸ κοινώσασθαί τέ μοι ἐπιχει-
ρεῖς καὶ ἀλλάξασθαι κάλλος ἀντὶ κάλλους,
οὐκ ὀλίγῳ μου πλεονεκτεῖν διανοῇ, ἀλλ᾽
ἀντὶ δόξης ἀλήθειαν καλῶν κτᾶσθαι ἐπιχει-
ρεῖς καὶ τῷ ὄντι "χρύσεα χαλκείων" διαμεί-
βεσθαι νοεῖς.

ἀλλ᾽, ὦ μακάριε, ἄμεινον σκόπει, μή σε
λανθάνω οὐδὲν ὤν. ἤ τοι τῆς διανοίας ὄψις
ἄρχεται ὀξὺ βλέπειν ὅταν ἡ τῶν ὀμμάτων
τῆς ἀκμῆς λήγειν ἐπιχειρῇ· σὺ δὲ τούτων ἔτι
πόρρω.

Ε. κἀγὼ ἀκούσας, τὰ μὲν παρ᾽ ἐμοῦ,
ἔφην, ταῦτά ἐστιν, ὧν οὐδὲν ἄλλως εἴρηται
ἢ ὡς διανοοῦμαι· σὺ δὲ αὐτὸς οὕτω βου-
λεύου ὅτι σοί τε ἄριστον καὶ ἐμοὶ ἡγῇ.

me an exceptional beauty, one far superior to your own good looks. If that were the case, in trying to exchange your beauty for mine you'd actually be aiming to get the better of me, because you'd be acquiring real beauty in exchange for superficial beauty. That would truly be "an exchange of gold for bronze."

So, my friend, take a closer look in case you'll find that I'm really not worth it. They say the mind's eye begins to see clearly when one's eyesight starts to fail, but you're still a long way off from that.

E. As far as I'm concerned, I replied, what I've said is simply what I think and feel. I'll leave it to you to figure out what's best for you and me.

ἀλλ᾽, ἔφη, τοῦτό γ᾽ εὖ λέγεις· ἐν γὰρ τῷ
ἐπιόντι χρόνῳ βουλευόμενοι πράξομεν ὃ ἂν
φαίνηται νῷν περί τε τούτων καὶ περὶ τῶν
ἄλλων ἄριστον.

ἐγὼ μὲν δὴ ταῦτα ἀκούσας τε καὶ εἰπών,
καὶ ἀφεὶς ὥσπερ βέλη, τετρῶσθαι αὐτὸν
ᾤμην· καὶ ἀναστάς γε, οὐδ᾽ ἐπιτρέψας
τούτῳ εἰπεῖν οὐδὲν ἔτι, ἀμφιέσας τὸ ἱμάτιον
τὸ ἐμαυτοῦ τοῦτον—καὶ γὰρ ἦν χειμών—
ὑπὸ τὸν τρίβωνα κατακλινεὶς τὸν τουτουί,
περιβαλὼν τὼ χεῖρε τούτῳ τῷ δαιμονίῳ ὡς
ἀληθῶς καὶ θαυμαστῷ, κατεκείμην τὴν
νύκτα ὅλην. καὶ οὐδὲ ταῦτα αὖ, ὦ Σώκρατες,
ἐρεῖς ὅτι ψεύδομαι. ποιήσαντος δὲ δὴ ταῦτα
ἐμοῦ οὗτος τοσοῦτον περιεγένετό τε καὶ
κατεφρόνησεν καὶ κατεγέλασεν τῆς ἐμῆς
ὥρας καὶ ὕβρισεν—καὶ περὶ ἐκεῖνό γε ᾤμην
τὶ εἶναι, ὦ ἄνδρες δικασταί· δικασταὶ γάρ
ἐστε τῆς Σωκράτους ὑπερηφανίας—εὖ γὰρ

Very well then, he said. In due course, we'll work out what's best in these and in other circumstances.

Following this exchange, I imagined that I'd aimed my arrows well and hit my target. I got up, and without letting him say another word I threw my cloak around him—it was wintertime—and lay down under his own threadbare garment. There I lay all night, with my arms wrapped around this mysterious and wonderful man—you can't deny any of this, Socrates—while he ignored everything I did. He was positively disdainful and dismissive of my beauty, which I thought had a lot going for it, gentlemen of the jury—yes, I'm making you the judge and jury of Socrates' haughty behavior. Let me tell you that when I awoke from having slept with Socrates—gods and

ἴστε μὰ θεούς, μὰ θεάς, οὐδὲν περιττότερον
καταδεδαρθηκὼς ἀνέστην μετὰ Σωκράτους,
ἢ εἰ μετὰ πατρὸς καθηῦδον ἢ ἀδελφοῦ
πρεσβυτέρου.

F. τὸ δὴ μετὰ τοῦτο τίνα οἴεσθέ με διά-
νοιαν ἔχειν, ἡγούμενον μὲν ἠτιμάσθαι,
ἀγάμενον δὲ τὴν τούτου φύσιν τε καὶ σω-
φροσύνην καὶ ἀνδρείαν, ἐντετυχηκότα
ἀνθρώπῳ τοιούτῳ οἵῳ ἐγὼ οὐκ ἂν ᾤμην
ποτ᾽ ἐντυχεῖν εἰς φρόνησιν καὶ εἰς καρτε-
ρίαν; ὥστε οὔθ᾽ ὅπως οὖν ὀργιζοίμην εἶχον
καὶ ἀποστερηθείην τῆς τούτου συνουσίας,
οὔτε ὅπῃ προσαγαγοίμην αὐτὸν ηὐπόρουν.
εὖ γὰρ ἤδη ὅτι χρήμασί γε πολὺ μᾶλλον
ἄτρωτος ἦν πανταχῇ ἢ σιδήρῳ ὁ Αἴας, ᾧ τε
ᾤμην αὐτὸν μόνῳ ἁλώσεσθαι, διεπεφεύγει
με. ἠπόρουν δή, καταδεδουλωμένος τε ὑπὸ
τοῦ ἀνθρώπου ὡς οὐδεὶς ὑπ᾽ οὐδενὸς ἄλλου
περιῇα.

goddesses are my witnesses—nothing more had happened than if I'd been sleeping with my father or older brother.

F. What do you suppose my frame of mind was after that? Of course, I felt I'd been snubbed, but at the same time I was in awe of his restraint and fortitude. I never imagined I'd encounter a man with such mental and physical resolve. As a result, I couldn't bring myself to be angry with him or renounce his company, though I had no hope of winning him over. I was well aware that he was as unconcerned about money as Ajax was indifferent to mortal combat, and that when I'd tried to ensnare him, in the only way I thought possible, he'd slipped through my fingers. I was at my wit's end, and more in thrall to Socrates than anyone has ever been to another person.

G. ταῦτά τε γάρ μοι ἅπαντα προυγεγόνει, καὶ μετὰ ταῦτα στρατεία ἡμῖν εἰς Ποτείδαιαν ἐγένετο κοινὴ καὶ συνεσιτοῦμεν ἐκεῖ. πρῶτον μὲν οὖν τοῖς πόνοις οὐ μόνον ἐμοῦ περιῆν, ἀλλὰ καὶ τῶν ἄλλων ἁπάντων— ὁπότ᾿ ἀναγκασθεῖμεν ἀποληφθέντες που, οἷα δὴ ἐπὶ στρατείας, ἀσιτεῖν, οὐδὲν ἦσαν οἱ ἄλλοι πρὸς τὸ καρτερεῖν—ἔν τ᾿ αὖ ταῖς εὐωχίαις μόνος ἀπολαύειν οἷός τ᾿ ἦν τά τ᾿ ἄλλα καὶ πίνειν οὐκ ἐθέλων, ὁπότε ἀναγκα- σθείη, πάντας ἐκράτει, καὶ ὃ πάντων θαυμα- στότατον, Σωκράτη μεθύοντα οὐδεὶς πώ- ποτε ἑώρακεν ἀνθρώπων. τούτου μὲν οὖν μοι δοκεῖ καὶ αὐτίκα ὁ ἔλεγχος ἔσεσθαι.

H. πρὸς δὲ αὖ τὰς τοῦ χειμῶνος καρτερήσεις—δεινοὶ γὰρ αὐτόθι

G. All this took place before we went on the expedition to Potidaea, where we shared digs together as messmates. In that situation, he outshone me and everyone else because of his ability to withstand the hardships of campaigning. When we were cut off from our supplies, as often happens in war, everyone else was hopeless at dealing with it; but equally, when we had a chance to indulge in fun and feasting, he was the only one who was really able to enjoy himself. And although he was not inclined to drink, when he was made to do so he could drink anyone under the table—and the extraordinary thing is that no man alive has ever seen Socrates drunk! I guess you'll be seeing proof of this soon enough.

H. The winters in that region are bitter, and Socrates' ability to put up with winter

χειμῶνες—θαυμάσια ἠργάζετο τά τε ἄλλα,
καί ποτε ὄντος πάγου οἵου δεινοτάτου,
καὶ πάντων ἢ οὐκ ἐξιόντων ἔνδοθεν, ἢ εἴ
τις ἐξίοι, ἠμφιεσμένων τε θαυμαστὰ δὴ ὅσα
καὶ ὑποδεδεμένων καὶ ἐνειλιγμένων τοὺς
πόδας εἰς πίλους καὶ ἀρνακίδας, οὗτος δ᾽ ἐν
τούτοις ἐξῄει ἔχων ἱμάτιον μὲν τοιοῦτον
οἷόνπερ καὶ πρότερον εἰώθει φορεῖν, ἀνυπό-
δητος δὲ διὰ τοῦ κρυστάλλου ῥᾷον ἐπορεύετο
ἢ οἱ ἄλλοι ὑποδεδεμένοι, οἱ δὲ στρατιῶται
ὑπέβλεπον αὐτὸν ὡς καταφρονοῦντα
σφῶν.

I. καὶ ταῦτα μὲν δὴ ταῦτα· "οἷον δ᾽ αὖ
τόδ᾽ ἔρεξε καὶ ἔτλη καρτερὸς ἀνὴρ"
[Homer, *Odyssey* 4.242] ἐκεῖ ποτε ἐπὶ στρα-
τιᾶς, ἄξιον ἀκοῦσαι. συννοήσας γὰρ αὐτόθι
ἕωθέν τι εἱστήκει σκοπῶν, καὶ ἐπειδὴ οὐ
προυχώρει αὐτῷ, οὐκ ἀνίει ἀλλὰ εἱστήκει
ζητῶν. καὶ ἤδη ἦν μεσημβρία, καὶ ἄνθρωποι

weather was incredible. When the frost was severe, the troops stayed under cover and only ventured out if they were thoroughly wrapped up and well shod, with their feet swathed in felt and fleeces. Socrates, however, would walk around among them wearing ordinary clothes, and would march across ice in bare feet more easily than the well-booted soldiers. They used to give him dirty looks, because they imagined he was viewing them with disdain.

I. That's one story. It's worth your hearing another one about "what this tough man fulfilled and did endure" while on campaign. One morning he'd been standing from the crack of dawn thinking about some problem, and when he couldn't work out the answer he didn't give up but stood there

ἠσθάνοντο, καὶ θαυμάζοντες ἄλλος ἄλλῳ
ἔλεγεν ὅτι Σωκράτης ἐξ ἑωθινοῦ φροντίζων
τι ἕστηκε. τελευτῶντες δέ τινες τῶν Ἰώνων,
ἐπειδὴ ἑσπέρα ἦν, δειπνήσαντες—καὶ γὰρ
θέρος τότε γ᾽ ἦν—χαμεύνια ἐξενεγκάμενοι
ἅμα μὲν ἐν τῷ ψύχει καθηῦδον, ἅμα δ᾽
ἐφύλαττον αὐτὸν εἰ καὶ τὴν νύκτα ἑστήξοι. ὁ
δὲ εἱστήκει μέχρι ἕως ἐγένετο καὶ ἥλιος
ἀνέσχεν· ἔπειτα ᾤχετ᾽ ἀπιὼν προσευξάμε-
νος τῷ ἡλίῳ.

J. εἰ δὲ βούλεσθε ἐν ταῖς μάχαις—τοῦτο
γὰρ δὴ δίκαιόν γε αὐτῷ ἀποδοῦναι—ὅτε
γὰρ ἡ μάχη ἦν ἐξ ἧς ἐμοὶ καὶ τἀριστεῖα
ἔδοσαν οἱ στρατηγοί, οὐδεὶς ἄλλος ἐμὲ
ἔσωσεν ἀνθρώπων ἢ οὗτος, τετρωμένον
οὐκ ἐθέλων ἀπολιπεῖν, ἀλλὰ συνδιέσωσε

thinking. By midday people had started to observe him with amazement, and word spread around that Socrates had been standing there meditating since daybreak. Finally, evening came, and after supper some Ionian troops brought out their sleeping-mats so that they could sleep in the open air—this was summertime—and to take the opportunity to watch him and see if he was going to stand there all night. Sure enough, he stood there until sunrise, and only when dawn broke did he offer a prayer to the sun and go on his way.

J. If you want to know how Socrates was in the midst of battle, and it would be only fair to tell you, let me describe the battle after which the commanders awarded a medal for bravery to me—although the man who saved my life was none other than Socrates.

καὶ τὰ ὅπλα καὶ αὐτὸν ἐμέ. καὶ ἐγὼ μέν, ὦ
Σώκρατες, καὶ τότε ἐκέλευον σοὶ διδόναι
τἀριστεῖα τοὺς στρατηγούς, καὶ τοῦτό γέ
μοι οὔτε μέμψῃ οὔτε ἐρεῖς ὅτι ψεύδομαι·
ἀλλὰ γὰρ τῶν στρατηγῶν πρὸς τὸ ἐμὸν
ἀξίωμα ἀποβλεπόντων καὶ βουλομένων
ἐμοὶ διδόναι τἀριστεῖα, αὐτὸς προθυμότε-
ρος ἐγένου τῶν στρατηγῶν ἐμὲ λαβεῖν ἢ
σαυτόν.

ἔτι τοίνυν, ὦ ἄνδρες, ἄξιον ἦν θεάσασθαι
Σωκράτη, ὅτε ἀπὸ Δηλίου φυγῇ ἀνεχώρει
τὸ στρατόπεδον· ἔτυχον γὰρ παραγενόμε-
νος ἵππον ἔχων, οὗτος δὲ ὅπλα. ἀνεχώρει
οὖν ἐσκεδασμένων ἤδη τῶν ἀνθρώπων
οὗτός τε ἅμα καὶ Λάχης· καὶ ἐγὼ περιτυγ-
χάνω, καὶ ἰδὼν εὐθὺς παρακελεύομαί τε
αὐτοῖν θαρρεῖν, καὶ ἔλεγον ὅτι οὐκ ἀπο-
λείψω αὐτώ.

He refused to leave me behind when I was wounded, and carried not just me but my armor to safety. On that occasion, I kept insisting to the commanders that they give you the award, Socrates—you can't fault me or say that's not true—but of course they wanted me to have the medal because they were conscious of my social standing. And you were even keener than they were that I and not you should have it.

Gentlemen, you should have seen how Socrates behaved on another occasion, when the army was fleeing from Delium. I was with the cavalry, he with the heavy infantry. The troops had already scattered and he was retreating with Laches. I ran into them, and as soon as I saw them, I shouted that they should keep going, and I promised I wouldn't abandon them.

Κ. ἐνταῦθα δὴ καὶ κάλλιον ἐθεασάμην Σωκράτη ἢ ἐν Ποτειδαίᾳ—αὐτὸς γὰρ ἧττον ἐν φόβῳ ἦ διὰ τὸ ἐφ᾽ ἵππου εἶναι—πρῶτον μὲν ὅσον περιῆν Λάχητος τῷ ἔμφρων εἶναι· ἔπειτα ἔμοιγ᾽ ἐδόκει, ὦ Ἀριστόφανες, τὸ σὸν δὴ τοῦτο, καὶ ἐκεῖ διαπορεύεσθαι ὥσπερ καὶ ἐνθάδε,

βρενθυόμενος καὶ τὠφθαλμὼ παραβάλ-λων, [Aristophanes, *Clouds* 362]

ἠρέμα παρασκοπῶν καὶ τοὺς φιλίους καὶ τοὺς πολεμίους, δῆλος ὢν παντὶ καὶ πάνυ πόρρωθεν ὅτι εἴ τις ἅψεται τούτου τοῦ ἀνδρός, μάλα ἐρρωμένως ἀμυνεῖται. διὸ καὶ ἀσφαλῶς ἀπῄει καὶ οὗτος καὶ ὁ ἑταῖρος· σχεδὸν γάρ τι τῶν οὕτω διακειμένων ἐν τῷ πολέμῳ οὐδὲ ἅπτονται, ἀλλὰ τοὺς προτρο-πάδην φεύγοντας διώκουσιν.

πολλὰ μὲν οὖν ἄν τις καὶ ἄλλα ἔχοι Σω-κράτη ἐπαινέσαι καὶ θαυμάσια· ἀλλὰ τῶν μὲν ἄλλων ἐπιτηδευμάτων τάχ᾽ ἄν τις καὶ περὶ

K. I had a better chance then of seeing Socrates in action than I had at Potidaea, since being on horseback meant I was personally in less danger. He was much calmer than Laches, loping along as he does in the city just as you described him, Aristophanes—

stalking like a pelican, stepping wide,
rolling his eyes from side to side.

He was coolly observing friend and foe, making it obvious to all, even from afar, that anyone who attacked him would meet fierce resistance. That's why he and his fellow-soldier got away safely. On the battlefield, pursuers generally don't go for men who behave like that. They chase after men who're frantically running away.

Well, I could find many things to say in praise of Socrates that would dazzle and impress you. One could probably say much

ἄλλου τοιαῦτα εἴποι, τὸ δὲ μηδενὶ ἀνθρώπων
ὅμοιον εἶναι, μήτε τῶν παλαιῶν μήτε τῶν
νῦν ὄντων, τοῦτο ἄξιον παντὸς θαύματος. [-]

the same kinds of thing about other people too, but the most extraordinary thing about Socrates is that he's unlike any person who's ever lived, past or present. [. . .]

FURTHER READING

Allan, William. 2014. *Classical Literature: A Very Short Introduction.* Oxford University Press.

Benardete, Seth. 2001. *Plato's Symposium: A Translation*, with commentaries by Allan Bloom and Seth Benardete. University of Chicago Press.

Blondell, Ruby. 2002. *The Play of Character in Plato's Dialogues.* Cambridge University Press.

D'Angour, Armand. 2019. *Socrates in Love: The Making of a Philosopher.* Bloomsbury.

Davidson, James. 2008. *The Greeks and Greek Love.* Weidenfeld and Nicolson.

Guthrie, W.K.C. 1975. *A History of Greek Philosophy.* Vol 4, *Plato, the Man and His Dialogues.* Cambridge University Press.

Hughes, Bettany. 2011. *The Hemlock Cup: Socrates, Athens and the Search for the Good Life.* Jonathan Cape.

Hunter, Richard. 2004. *Plato's Symposium.* Oxford University Press.

Lear, Jonathan. 1999. *Open Minded: Working Out the Logic of the Soul.* Harvard University Press.

Lesher, J., Debra Nails, and Frisbee Sheffield, eds. 2006. *Plato's Symposium: Issues in Interpretation and Reception.* Center for Hellenic Studies.

May, Simon. 2011. *Love: A History.* Yale University Press.

Nehamas, Alexander, and Paul Woodruff. 1989. *Plato, Symposium.* Hackett Publishing.

Nussbaum, Martha. 1986. *The Fragility of Goodness.* Cambridge University Press.

Rowe, Christopher. 1998. *Plato: Symposium.* Aris and Phillips.

Rowe, Christopher. 2005. *Plato: Phaedrus.* Penguin.

Scott, Gary Alan, and William A. Welton. 2008. *Erotic Wisdom: Philosophy and Intermediacy in Plato's Symposium.* State University of New York Press.

Sheffield, Frisbee. 2006. *Plato's Symposium: The Ethics of Desire.* Oxford University Press.

Waterfield, Robin. 2009. *Why Socrates Died: Dispelling the Myths.* W. W. Norton & Company.

West, M. L., trans. 1999. *Greek Lyric Poetry: The Poems and Fragments of the Greek Iambic, Elegiac, and Melic Poets (Excluding Pindar and Bacchylides) down to 450 B.C.* Clarendon Press.

CONCORDANCE TO PASSAGES SELECTED

The complete Greek text is standardly paginated according to the sixteenth-century edition of Plato edited by Henri Estienne (Stephanus), with page, section, and line numbers. *Symposium* begins at 172a1 and ends at 223d11.

SPEAKER	PAGES	SECTIONS	GREEK TEXT
Phaedrus	(6–19)	A–E	178a5–180b8
Pausanias	(26–39)	A–E	180c3–181d6
		F	183d5–183e5
		G	184c3–184e4
		H	185b4–185c2
Eryximachus	(44–59)	A–I	186a2–188d7
Aristophanes	(66–79)	A–E	189d5–191d4,
			192e7–193b2

CONCORDANCE TO PASSAGES SELECTED

SPEAKER	PAGES	SECTIONS	GREEK TEXT
Agathon	(84–93)	A–C	195a7–197a5
		D–E	197c3–197e5
Socrates	(106–125)	A–B	204a1–204c6
		C	206a9–206d2
		D–G	210a3–212a6
Alcibiades	(134–159)	A–K	217c6–221d4